These Mad Hybrids

John Hoyland and Contemporary Sculpture

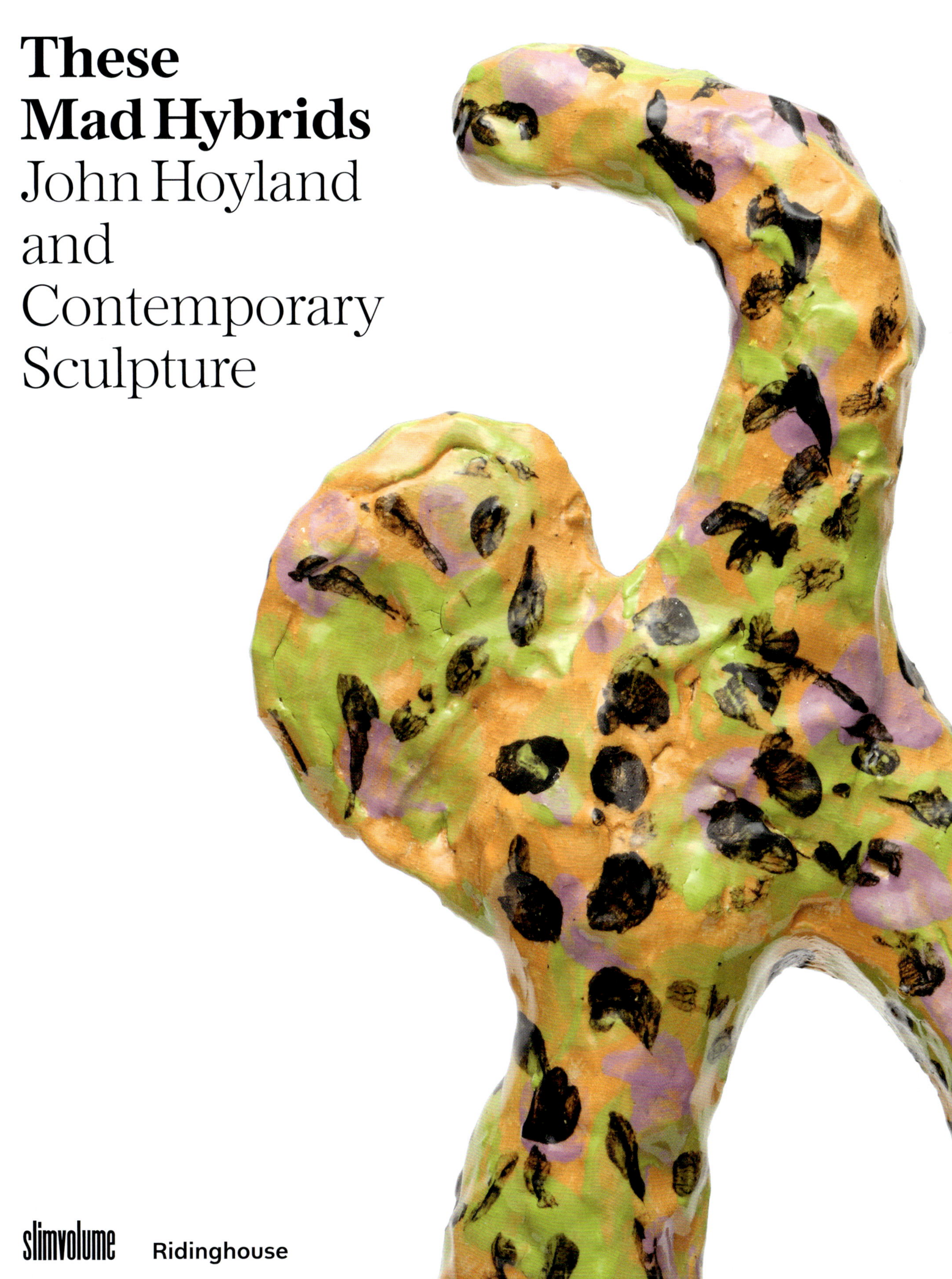

These
Mad Hybrids

John Hoyland and Contemporary Sculpture

slimvolume Ridinghouse

Contents

John Hoyland's Ceramics:
Throwing Wild Shapes
Andrew Hunt

7

Constructing Painting, Imagining Sculpture:
John Hoyland's Ceramics in Context
Sam Cornish

13

Ceramics

27

These Mad Hybrids:
John Hoyland's Ceramics and Contemporary Sculpture
Olivia Bax

53

Exhibition

63

It was Beauty that Killed the Beast
James Fisher

109

Shifting Surfaces:
Selections from John Hoyland's Photographic Archive
Hannah Hughes

113

Photographic Credits

124

Artist Biographies

126

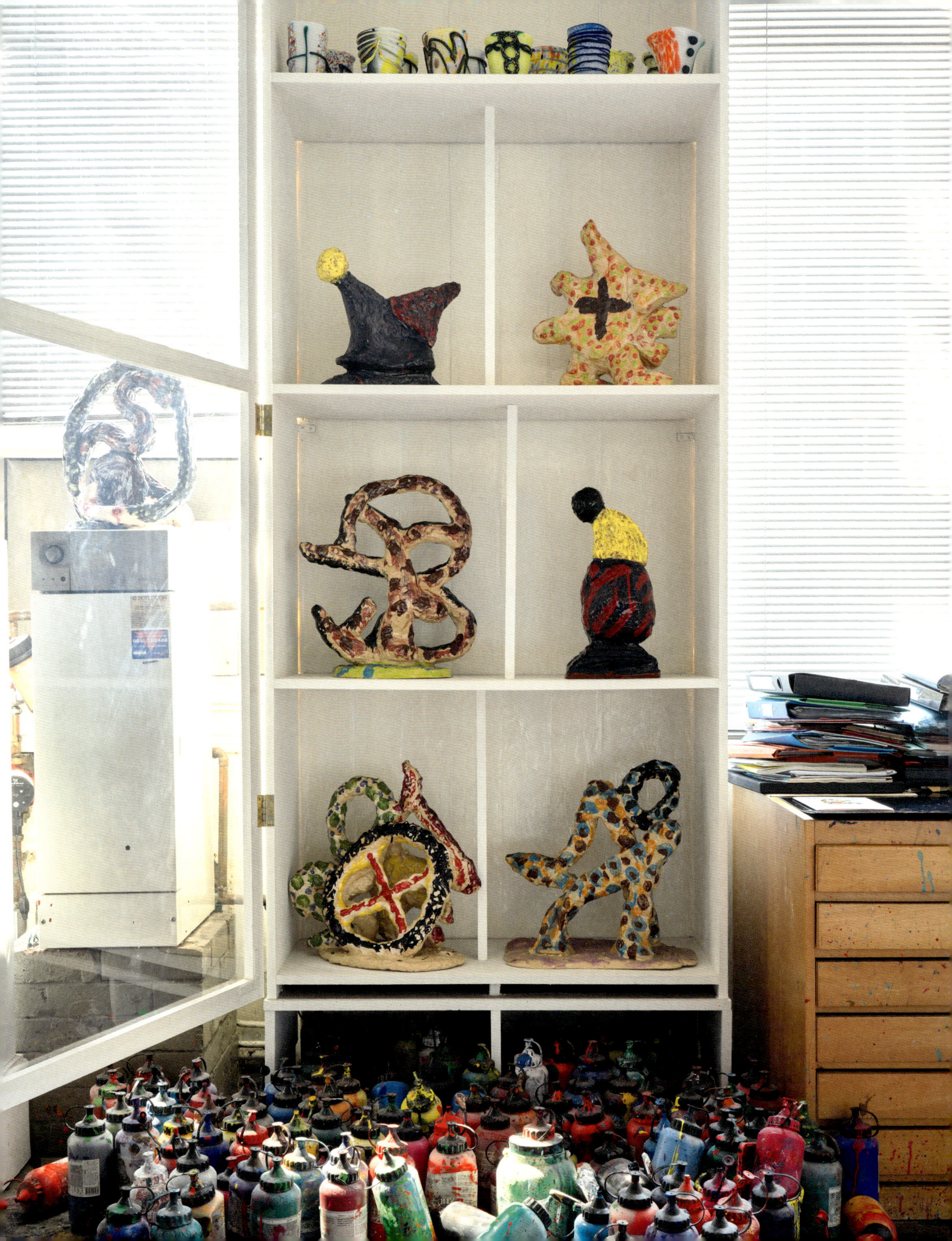

John Hoyland's Ceramics: Throwing Wild Shapes

Andrew Hunt

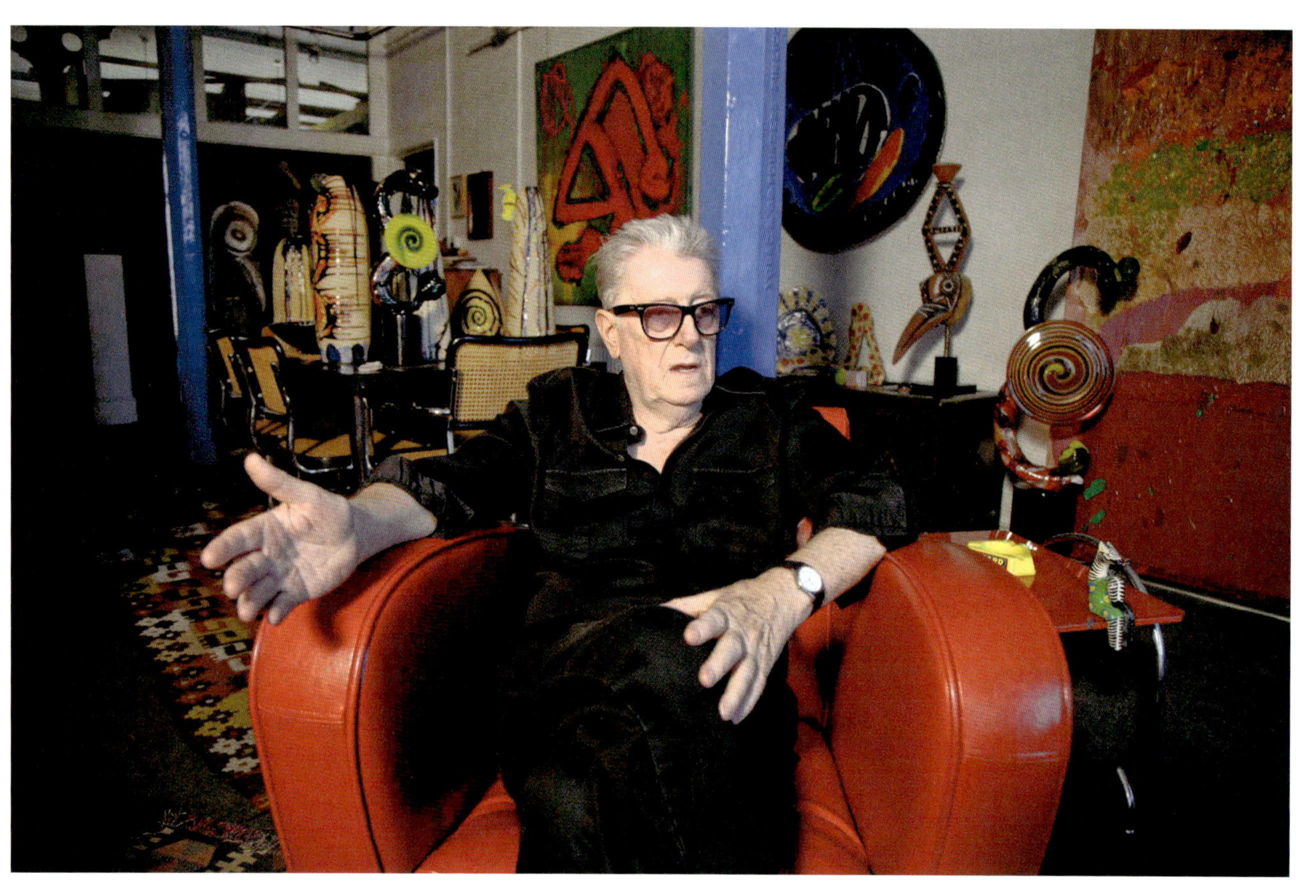

John Hoyland, photographed by
Derrick Santini, 2009

In a recent documentary on his life in the rock band the Rolling Stones, Keith Richards describes the moment he developed the chord structure for the classic track 'Gimme Shelter' (1969). Playing through his preferred tuning of open G – a simple device allowing for easy improvisation within barred chord progression – he says: 'There's something about the intonation, the separation; it's almost mystical. Hit in the right way in the right moment, you know…*cheap ride to heaven*'.[1]

Hearing Richards's variation of notes – emphasised further at the moment Charlie Watts's drums drop in and the subsequent effect of Richards's overdubbed guitar licks – made me think of how the best in painting and its expanded field can provide a similar unorthodox state of grace, comparable goosebumps or *jouissance* associated with effective circular scores in popular music written since 1966.[2] However, it is not often we feel this in galleries in the 2020s. In fact, it is rare that we feel this in art at all. Consider this: when did you last hook a cheap ride to heaven in your local art centre? Furthermore, when did you even consider this a possibility?

For me, against the odds, this happens with the English painter John Hoyland's highly eccentric ceramic works from 1994. Formed 'in the right way, at the right moment' – as a counterpoint to, and in combination with, a 'right kind of wrong', through a deliberately informal approach to sculpture – Hoyland's objects achieve something akin to a rhythm that is refreshingly alien. These colourfully playful quasi-domestic ornaments' balance of camp intonation and separation (light and dark, silence and noise, figurative indolence and accidental gesture) achieve something unusually electrifying. The ultimate rapture lies in their 'hybridity', between a reflexivity in thinking and feeling that results in a 'mad' cadence. And I mean 'mad' in the very best sense of the word: 'enthusiastic', 'ridiculous', 'preposterous'.

It is important to mention that Hoyland's three-dimensional works were shown to me for the first time by Olivia Bax, Sam Cornish and Beverley Heath-Hoyland at The John Hoyland Estate in Farringdon, London, in the summer of 2023, when we discussed the production of this book ahead of the touring exhibition in which it plays a central part. As Olivia said to me at the time, Hoyland described these specific works as 'mad hybrids'. Like Pablo Picasso's clay renditions of painted surfaces, they appear playfully childlike in their loose execution. Hoyland's only other previous ceramic works had been made when he was about 11 years old, and Sam's comprehensive biographical text shows the artist's obsession with plasticine and glitter wax as a child, which adds to the deliberately naive aspect of this work.

Another text, James Fisher's 'It was Beauty that Killed the Beast', provides an unconventional reading of Hoyland's work, this time with King Kong acting as a metaphor for hybridity: of man and beast, a mixture of rational and instinctive creativity. Fisher cites the American musician Daniel Johnson's song 'Kong' from 1983. Importantly, Johnson was a significant figure in the outsider, lo-fi and alternative music scenes of the 1980s and 1990s, and had a similar innocent approach to making. Personally speaking, I own a drawing by Johnson and it seems appropriate to mention it here: the work shows a small shape-shifting figure below the caption 'become something else'. This character has a parallel identity to the transformative nature of Hoyland's three-dimensional works.

Like the works of other painters and discordant music from the same period of Picasso's ceramics in the early twentieth century – think of Henri Matisse's works as sophisticated graphic design with compulsive underpainting or 'pentimenti', an admission of 'getting it wrong' and a subsequent 'repenting' of one's sins, or the offbeat timing and economy of discordant rhythm in Igor Stravinsky as a precursor for conceptual blues – Hoyland's ceramics contain a clearly developed underlying structure alongside a wilfully guileless mode of progression that informs the pace and tempo of his series.

Thupelo Memory, *The World* and *Sorcerer* (all 1994), for example, on first view, immediately dance in an ostentatious and carefree manner. They are three-dimensional equivalents to the ridiculous cockerel postures Mick Jagger made to the musical composition mentioned above. Hoyland's ceramics not only throw similar wild shapes[3] to those of Jagger, but they also 'perform' a devil-may-care demonstration of rhythm in time and space, a dance designed to liberate us. As we look at them in the mid-2020s they are wonderfully free from mannered tropes of conduct in contemporary sculpture and painting.

They are also firm precursors for artists who work with ceramics that have emerged and energised us in the past 15 years: for example, Aaron Angell, an artist who has had a huge impact on the medium in the UK and has acted as a facilitator for others through his founding of the Troy Town Art Pottery in east London. Many painters of course have used ceramics in disorderly or counter-intuitive ways at various points in their careers across contemporary history. These include Julian Schnabel (from the very beginning), Mary Heilmann and Allison Katz. There is a combination of the impish and the serious in all three of these artists' work. To push the musical trope further, Katz has an ongoing interest in cockerels in her work, which in many respects act as humorous feminist symbols: a form of 'funny feminism' evident in the oeuvre of painters such as Amy Sillman and Laura Owens, who laugh at defensive posturing in male painting.

Beyond this, it can be claimed that Hoyland's 'mad hybrids' operate in a less insecure manner too, and function in the historical canon as a humorous synthesis of styles that goes beyond modern and ironic postmodern painting. This provides another 'pre-post-erous'[4] angle of interpretation, meaning both 'pre' and 'post' simultaneously, a 'funny' art historical knight's move that confounds the usual art historical straitjacket of chronological progression. We can see this clearly in the work of Merlin Carpenter (the foremost arch-ironic critical-postmodern painter in the UK today) and his attempt to display his own copies of Hoyland's early 1960s abstract paintings in a solo exhibition during 2017 at the Simon Lee Gallery, London. When asked for permission some years before his death in 2011, Hoyland said 'no' to Carpenter, who went on to show his copies anyway, covered in cardboard. Hoyland comes out on top in this bizarre, alienated game of one-upmanship, namely because his paintings trump Carpenter's ego-defensive position involving market critique.[5] Through Hoyland's innately relaxed informality or use of productive non-sense, his work disrupts the overly rational regime of conservative postmodern irony, simply serving to confound it.

Moreover, Hoyland's ceramics serve to demystify his own painting not only for a wider audience, but also against purists of abstract theory. Ultimately, we realise, through looking at these works, that they are motifs that coexist in the artist's abstract canvases, and that both his paintings and ceramics can be deciphered through their relationship with the artist's photographs. It turns out that there is an archive of Polaroids by Hoyland that show images of mundane detritus and graffiti on the street. This was Hoyland's source material (see Hannah Hughes's visual essay pp.113–123) for many of the wonderful motifs in his paintings and sculpture from the 1980s onwards: silhouettes that contain an explicit humanity connected to their earthy, sometimes abject 'everyday' sources. This triangulation of photography, painting and sculpture, between 'thesis', 'antithesis' and 'synthesis' (a Hegelian basis for historical progression in discourse previously confounded in the story enacted by Carpenter between modernism, postmodernism and productive non-sense), this time works on a purely formal level to help render Hoyland's abstract pieces familiar and representational (a real triangle, for example, also exists in the case of *Thupelo Memory*). Again, this fact serves to resist any easy chronological art historical positioning of Hoyland's work. His is an economic practice that, through a circular progression or loop between photography, painting and sculpture, between representation and abstraction, between modernism, postmodernism and back again, becomes 'transcendental'. This is the basic structure for Hoyland's own 'cheap ride to heaven'.

Finally, it is important to mention that the work *Sorcerer* holds a wider performative clue to the final section of Hoyland's life and for this book as a whole. For me, this is a self-conscious nod to the final period of the artist's career, pitted in a theatrically autobiographical manner. *The Tempest*, of course, was a metaphor for William Shakespeare's own life. The playwright's last dramatic piece depicts Prospero, an exiled magician, breaking his staff as a final renunciation of magic. In turn, *Sorcerer* is the start of Hoyland's own impish goodbye. While Hoyland was far from the end in 1994, one can claim that he had made his 'major' contribution to painting by that time and was mature enough to start throwing caution to the wind.

In essence, this book and the art in it make a significant contribution to knowledge in both painting and ceramics, connected to previously unseen or relatively unknown work by a major British artist. Such work has the ability to contribute to new readings of art history, and it is the hope of the people involved in this publication that it provides a small but important example of an artist working productively between the lines. It is in this spirit that I would like to thank Olivia Bax and Sam Cornish for their original research in this book and for their intellectual rigour, energy and enthusiasm for John Hoyland's oeuvre. I would also like to thank Sophie Kullmann for introducing me to Sam and Olivia, and for managing the entire production of this publication. Additional thanks go to Wiz Patterson Kelly for her invaluable assistance at Hoyland Studio, Mike Dyer for his beautiful book design, James Fisher, Angus Pryor and Andrew Bick from the University of Gloucestershire for their support, and most of all to Beverley Heath-Hoyland for her constant and unwavering support of John Hoyland's entire project.

1   From *My Life as a Rolling Stone Episode II: Keith Richards*. Director: Oliver Murray. Air date: 2 July 2022, BBC iPlayer.

2   The year 1966 is an important one according to the writer Jon Savage. In *1966: The Year the Decade Exploded*, Faber & Faber, London, 2015, Savage describes a shift in popular music, in which circular movement becomes increasingly evident in place of linear scores or chronological progression in music. Examples include The Beatles' 'Tomorrow Never Knows', which famously uses non-Western influences to create a looped musical structure, and is included on the 1966 album, tellingly titled *Revolver*.

3   This comment and the title of this foreword owes a debt to Amy Sillman's paper 'Notes on Shape', which was presented at the symposium 'Painting: Funny Peculiar' at Manchester School of Art on 6 June 2019 (subsequently published by Slimvolume as a book under the same name in 2020), which was followed by Sillman's exhibition *The Shape of Shape* at MoMA, New York, 21 October 2019 to 4 October 2020.

4   It is important to mention that the critic and historian Hal Foster and the critic Robert Garnett have previously used the idea of the 'pre-post-erous' in different ways. The first art historically in relation to the work of Jeremy Deller; the second in relation to contemporary art and humour.

5   For more on 'anally retentive, ego-defensive' positions in contemporary painting connected to the legacy of postmodern irony, see Robert Garnett's essay 'Beyond Irony: Humour, Painting and the Funny-Peculiar', in Andrew Hunt (ed.), *Painting: Funny Peculiar*, Slimvolume, London, 2020, pp.68–83.

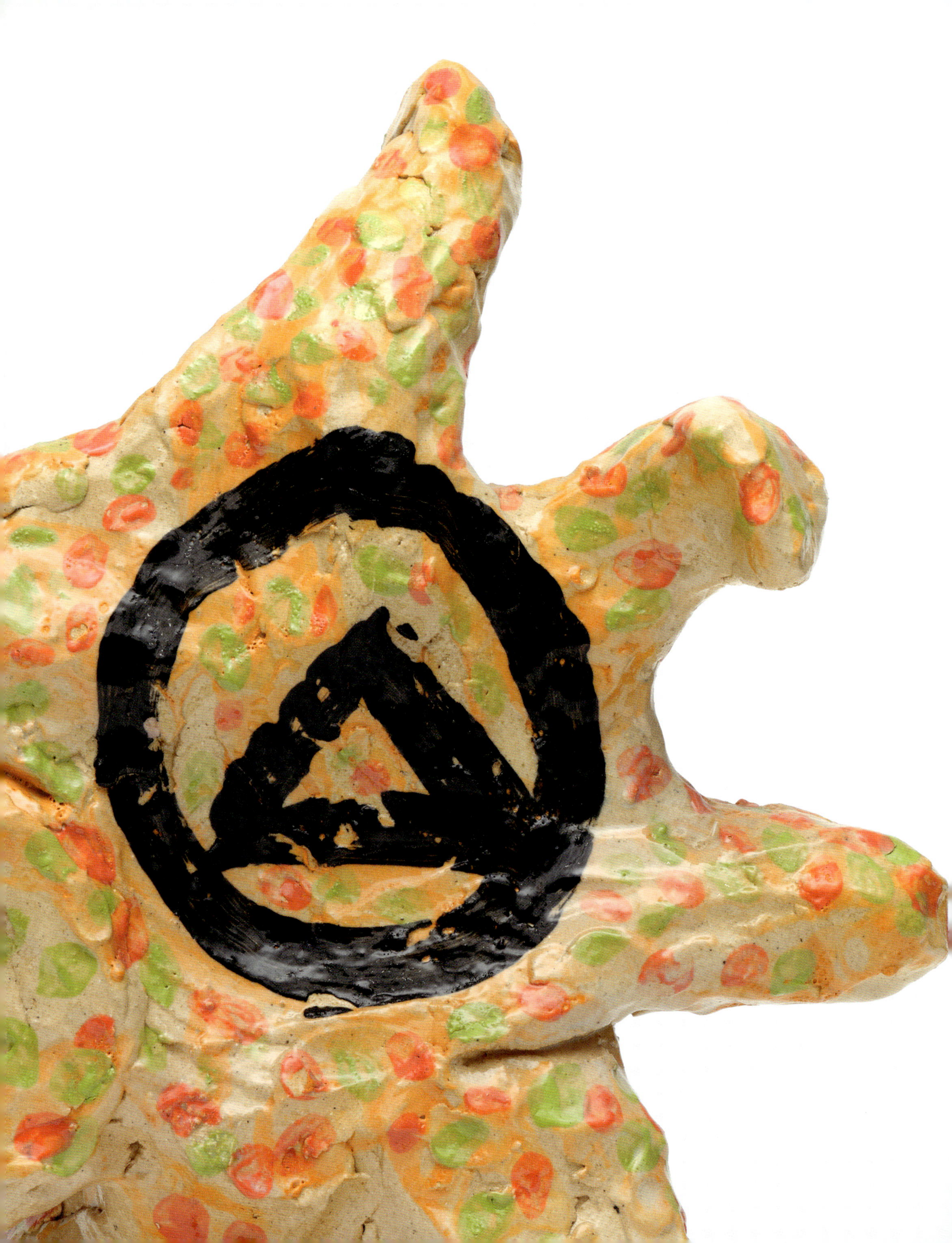

Constructing Painting, Imagining Sculpture: John Hoyland's Ceramics in Context

Sam Cornish

Sculpture was an early fascination of John Hoyland's. His mother Kathleen remembered the 'hours and hours you spent as a small boy, fashioning tiny figures not more than 2" tall, but their clothes etc., correct in every detail, and all done in plasticine, or as this became scarce, glitter wax. You used to have them climbing twigs in lieu of trees'. At the junior art school in Sheffield he modelled and painted a group of ceramic figurines (see p.29), a 'jockey ready to mount the horse, a smith shoeing a horse, a horse lying down etc.; the Indian Brave with tomahawk, Bishop, Prehistorical animal'.[1] Moving to Sheffield College of Art in 1951, Hoyland opted for stone-carving, although fairly quickly gave it up:

> *It was so boring, they used to sit us in this cellar of the old college and me and a guy called Terry Lee had these huge lumps of soft stone, like cheese. We didn't know what the hell we were doing and we just used to knock these big lumps off and try to make a seated female; I suppose one had a vague idea of a Henry Moore.[2]*

Almost four decades later, Hoyland embarked on his first and only concentrated sculpture-making project as a mature artist. The result was a group of 25 ceramic sculptures (see pp.26–51). They were commissioned by Christie's Contemporary Art (CCA) and completed in the first half of 1994, a period when he made no paintings on canvas.[3] There were other objects, before and after, in the 1980s and later 1990s, and shortly after the millennium. He painted plates, platters, vases and a series of vessels thrown by potter Dan Kelly, and on two occasions worked with master glass-blower Giovanni Tieuli in Murano, Venice. The products of these collaborations pick up on a stylishness and attraction to display and pleasure that is a consistent element in his art, and his attitude to life. The same is true of the 1994 ceramic sculptures, yet they add something else to the mix, partly formal variety and conviction, and partly a distinct, if defiantly ambiguous content.

Domestic-scaled, covered in wonky improvised patterns, the ceramic sculptures can sit on a side table or become a dinner-party centre-piece, but maybe not very comfortably, drawing attention to themselves and rewarding close looking with their individualised and provocative physical presences. Enjoyment and decoration meet something richer and perhaps in some cases darker, bringing the ceramics more fully into the main body of Hoyland's art, while emphasising its anarchic edge and ever-changing engagement with sculpture and the sculptural. The bulging shape and wiggling line of some paintings of 1962–63 were partly based upon an illustration of a Chinese vase or lamp, an early instance of his attraction to non-Western art forms, as well as of his use of images of objects as prompts for paintings, an approach he used much more widely in the 1980s and 1990s.[4] The ceramics could be seen as decoration released from its function of overlaying or modulating an underlying structure, and given its own thickly physical structural independence. It is as if the elaborate handles or spouts of china plates or vessels had broken free and acquired their own independent life. Decoration can imply harmony, order and comfort but because of these qualities can quickly veer into the excessive and uncontainable.

The best of Hoyland's paintings tend to be large in size and large in feel. The relatively small ceramics have a surprising, if slightly absurd, monumentality, an expression of confidence and control that also seems self-mocking, simultaneously employing and parodying the epic scale he used with great flair. This is an aspect of the irony and even humour he found in them, which he did not approach so directly elsewhere in his art. Humour also comes from the sense that each of the ceramics is an individual creature with a distinct, antic personality. He called them his

I was never really drawn to Renaissance Art – my secret loves were the archaic world and the arts of other cultures, Egyptian, Indian, Polynesian and African, which were largely considered to be 'Primitive Art' until this century. Many of these influences were absorbed by the Modern Masters, Picasso, Matisse and Brancusi during the 1920s.

I had not touched three-dimensional ceramics since I was seven years old until I began this group of work at the Royal College of Art this year. After my initial optimism at the 'idea' of the project I began to realise that it was harder than it looked, but guided and encouraged by David Harrison we produced this group of work. It's too early for me to gauge how I feel about it. What I really enjoyed was the freedom to 'try anything', the unexpected results with some of the colour, and also to indulge in the possibility of introducing irony and even humour into these mad little hybrids.

John Hoyland
May 1994

John Hoyland, text from the CCA
exhibition pamphlet: *John Hoyland:
Ceramic Works*, 1994, CCA Galleries,
London, 1–25 June 1994

Fig.1

'three-dimensional monsters', unconsciously (or not) following Joan Miró's designation of his own sculptures as a 'phantasmagoric world of living monsters'.[5] Hoyland once expressed admiration for Jann Haworth's 'strange dolls…quite menacing things', words that well describe the ceramics themselves.[6] A contemporary magazine presented them as a 'new troupe of 3-D figures', containing 'tenticular writhings, humorous intestines, a cross between Pulchinello [*Punchinello*] and a giraffe'.[7] We are perhaps in the company of a grotesque version of a *commedia dell'arte*, a popular subject for ceramicists of earlier centuries, with its flamboyantly costumed figures, caught in arrested theatrical motion.

When novelist Howard Jacobson visited Hoyland's studio and apartment in 2006, he encountered a group of Dan Kelly's upright ceramic vessels, fluidly painted by Hoyland. 'Great phallic excrescences', they occupied the dining table to the complete exclusion of potential guests (see p.8). Acknowledging that Hoyland was a 'man of appetite and indulgence', Jacobson attributed the apparent refusal to entertain to an inherent restlessness, the impression Hoyland gave of not being content to 'inhabit only one dimension at a time'.[8] This restlessness, artistic as well as personal, is fundamental to Hoyland's paintings, driving what Philip Dodd has recently recognised as its dialectical progression, its mutation from year to year, decade to decade.[9] It is shown in concentrated form in the 1994 ceramics, which Hoyland called 'these mad little hybrids' (fig.1).

The ceramics' hybridity, their restless embrace of different states of being, is expressed in their mixture of painting and sculpture; sculpture and decoration; colour and physical form; abstraction and figuration; animate and inanimate forms; tightly controlled structure and a seemingly soft shapelessness. At times they suggest a gleeful and gloopy sexuality, gaudily ornamented. The most compelling combine spatial definiteness with a sense we are witnessing them caught on the cusp of change, whether a temporary rearrangement as they lurch, stride or grasp, or a more absolute change of identity. An initial impression of formlessness, blobby and lumpen, only partially disguises an underlying tautness, a sense of physical resistance that is in part rooted in their employment of geometric structures, providing 'solidity and fantasy in equal measure'.[10]

Hybridity of a different sort can also be found in Hoyland's engagement with African and Oceanic sculpture, of which he was an occasional collector.[11] 'I was never really drawn to Renaissance Art – my secret loves were the archaic world and the arts of other cultures, Egyptian, Indian, Polynesian and African, which were largely considered to be "Primitive Art" until this century' (see fig.1). The tripod and cupped-bowl base of *Imaginary Being* (p.38) follows a large sculpture of a bird from New Guinea (p.28) displayed in his apartment, near the door to the studio.[12] From the 1980s onwards he hoped to create what he called 'new hybrids', cross-cultural forms, an artistic 'Esperanto', although one he realised was perhaps just as doomed to failure.[13] Trying to fully pin down the elements of their hybridity will always fall somewhat short. Mixed messages invite personal, idiosyncratic interpretation. Hoyland's friend, the Catalan artist Guillem Ramos-Poquí, wrote to him shortly after encountering them for the first time, describing: 'A hybrid camouflage of primordial anthropomorphical forms & "tasty" French patisserie. Rich in polysemic multi-layered significations: the celebration of glorious erotic anal explorations and palatable exotic tastes is interwoven with memories of ancient Minoan snake goddesses, symbols of fertility and embryonic metamorphosis'.[14]

Hoyland made the ceramics at the Royal College of Art, assisted by a student, David Harrison. The previous year, Maggi Hambling was the first painter to take up the CCA sculpture commission.[15] In their tubular construction and their creatureliness, Hoyland's ceramics seem aware of Hambling's, although with the brash strength of their colour, their often glossy finish and their physical robustness, they appear as indirect criticism of the powder-dry fresco-like hues and physical fragility of her examples. There are hints of a shared iconography as well: an eye floats ambiguously across some of the ceramics made by both artists. But Hoyland's ceramics can be found prefigured within his art in general, their imagery traced to the paintings he had made in the dozen years that preceded them.

The triangles of *Ocean Man*, *Fauna* and *Animal Imagined* (see pp.42, 49, 48) relate to Hoyland's paintings of 1982–83, a pivotal period of his art, while the thickly entwining lines of *Warrior*, *Thupelo Memory*, *Sorcerer* and *Roots* (see pp.51, 47, 50) follow the calligraphic drawing-in-space of the 'sky-writing' paintings of 1988–91.[16] The titles of the ceramic sculptures *Lamia*, *Warrior*, *Animal Imagined*, *Sorcerer* and *Benton* (see pp.40, 51, 48, 50, 33) are among those that repeat titles of paintings from the previous 12 years; those of *Thupelo Memory* and *Bablaz* (p.32) (South African slang for a hangover) connect to his recent experience at a workshop in Thupelo, near Johannesburg, in 1992, as perhaps do *Fauna* and *Roots*, given that at the workshop he drew 'plants and rocks and pick-up things'.[17] The iridescent paints Hoyland first used at Thupelo may have alterted him to the potential for glazes to enhance the sense of movement in his ceramic sculptures.[18]

Prior to the current exhibition, the ceramics have only been shown once, in June 1994 at CCA's London gallery. Apart from the CCA price list, I have found no comprehensive record of them. The CCA list includes 23 sculptures, out of 25, so the group of 21 owned by his widow Beverley Heath-Hoyland is likely to be near complete. Only six can be conclusively associated with their titles (*Warrior*, *Thupelo Memory*, *Sorcerer*, *Animal Im-*

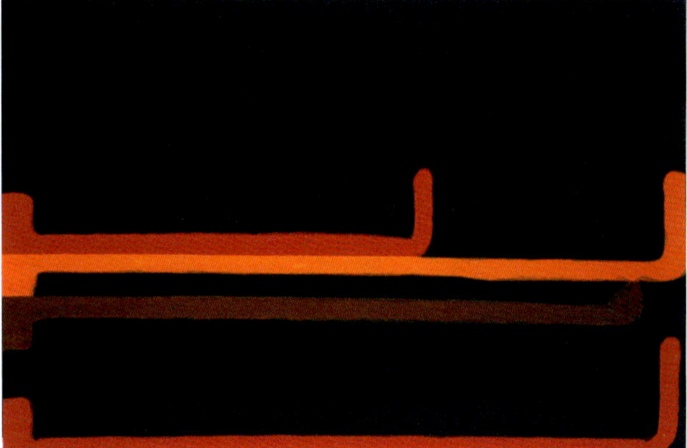

John Hoyland, *25.6.66*, 1966
Acrylic on canvas, 168 × 274 cm

agined, *Lamia*, *Maverick*); the others I have matched to the CCA list through a process of more-or-less inspired guesswork.[19] For many years before Hoyland's death in 2011 they occupied a prominent place in his London studio, displayed in two specially made cabinets, with two or three others positioned in the adjoining apartment (see pp.6, 26, 30–31). The ceramics he made at junior art school were kept, in more cramped conditions, on an adjacent shelf. Hoyland referred to his schoolboy works in his introduction to the CCA exhibition, and we can see some evidence of his looking back in the ceramics themselves. The New Guinea-inspired base of *Imaginary Being* bulges like the horse's hoofs in the schoolboy ceramics. Melanesian mythology meets a childhood image of a disappearing rural English life, overlapping motifs at different cultural, spatial and temporal distances.

The only mature sculptures made by the painter, the ceramics stand to one side of the main thrust of his output, oddities that revel in their oddness. Yet in many ways they fit into the development of Hoyland's art.

In their strange animation, their biomorphism and their humour, they amplify the latent Surrealism of his paintings of the early to mid-1960s. This phase of his endeavour was partially influenced by the sculpture of his friends Phillip King and William Tucker, which had its own Surrealist undertones, a sense of enigma and unsettling surprise, albeit wrapped in laconic geometric form. In 1967 Bryan Robertson suggested 'there is a double-take of one kind or another in every Hoyland painting, as if an object and its reflection were dislocated from logical alignment'.[20] This seems a useful description of the multi-limbed, baseball mitt of *Dragon* (pp.36–37), suggesting the way it moves in more than one direction at once, and how its two-part decorative scheme simultaneously articulates and confuses our sense of an underlying physical structure. The blocks of colour in Hoyland's paintings of 1964–65 often seem alive, part boulder, part alien life form; Robert Melville saw them as having 'equivocal reasons for being there, as if they had just alighted and were about to start a reconnaissance'.[21] Melville's description also nicely figures the ceramics as a group, hinting at their ambiguous agency and their straddling of more than one plane of existence. It is possible to imagine the squished blocks of paintings such as *15.5.64* (1964) or the tendril-like forms of *25.6.66* (1966, fig.2) as the long-dormant raw material from which the ceramics were created three decades later, somehow extracted from the 'dream-space' of Hoyland's early colour-fields and given three-dimensional existence.[22]

Fast-forward a decade and a half to the early 1980s, the years when Hoyland broke with transatlantic High Modernism. This optimistic and rigorous attitude to art, stemming from American Abstract Expressionism and Post-Painterly Abstraction, had provided the context for his paintings since the mid-1960s. Part of Hoyland's contribution to High Modernism was to bring a sculptural definiteness and solidity to an attitude to art rooted in a fluid, fast-moving, quickly apprehended visuality. His engagement with the abstract sculpture of his great friend Anthony Caro was important, with Caro's formal clarity helping to contain the referential ambiguity of Hoyland's images of the earlier 1960s. High Modernism gave Hoyland room to create a distinctive, if ever-changing style, and develop an international reputation. But in the early 1980s he sought new types of physicality, new types of pictorial structures and, most significantly, a new relationship between his images and the wider world, one which was partly mediated by sculpture, as well as by a broad variety of objects with potentially potent sculptural power. He reflected: 'I realised that artists with the greatest imagination and invention need to be stimulated not only intellectually but through the external world. Miró went on the beach every day and collected shells, bric-a-brac, whatever had washed up. Moore picked up stones, flints and shards'.[23]

As Hoyland threw off the productive restrictions of High Modernism, with its concentration on the formal characteristics of art and its belief that art largely came from art, his images broadened, became more complex, ushering in a more pronounced and in many ways more troubling physicality. A succession of paintings based around motifs of stacked triangles were the first outcome of this shift, followed by his circle paintings of 1983–85.

Triangular motifs had been prevalent in Hoyland's paintings of 1980–82, used to dynamically and inventively arrange images that are experienced primarily visually, with swathes of colour suspended in complex vistas of light, space and air. The paintings from May 1982 onwards have a very different character. Shining in subterranean darkness, the triangles in paintings such as *Master of Revels 6.8.82* (fig.3) or *King of Misrule 15.8.82* (both 1982) have an independent and somewhat crude solidity, with one placed on top of another, 'stones, flints and shards' enlarged to monumental proportions. Significantly, these stacked sculptural units at times suggest distinct personages. A mountain-like triangle merges together different symbols for human presence: simultaneously head and face, helmet, crown and dunce's cap; all balanced on bases that imply a combination of legs, feet and body. We look into a Hoyland painting of early 1982, experiencing its sense of freedom and release. The paintings post May 1982 almost seem to look back at us, projecting an uncertain expression that mixes absurdity, boisterousness, heroism, insolence and a kind of defiance. The ceramics, having been pulled out of the limited space of painting, extend this connection between absurdity, sculptural solidity, and an active and provocative presence. This is most clearly shown in the eyes daubed onto *Ocean Man* (p.42) or *Ruler* (p.43), the party hat cheekily perched on top of *Benton* (p.33), or in the dunce's caps of *Bablaz* (p.32), *Enigma* (p.48), *Doppie* (p.48) and *Conjuror* (pp.34–35).

Pablo Picasso became an important influence on Hoyland's paintings of the 1980s, and on the ceramics themselves. The circle paintings (see, for example, fig.4) – 'deliberately over-loaded with allusive referential ambiguities' – draw on the metaphoric potential central to Picasso's vision.[24] Mel Gooding saw in the circle paintings 'a glutinous thickness that recalls the passionate lubricity of late Picasso'.[25] Hoyland could equally be seen as drawing on the constructed aspects of Picasso's painting, the overwhelming

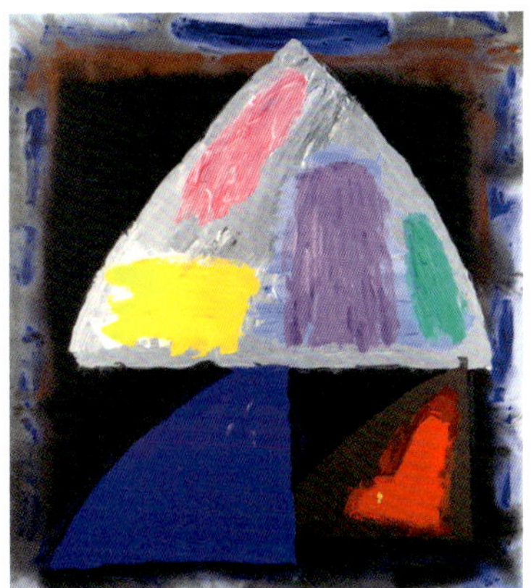

John Hoyland, *Master of Revels 6.8.82*, 1982
Acrylic on canvas, 257 × 231 cm

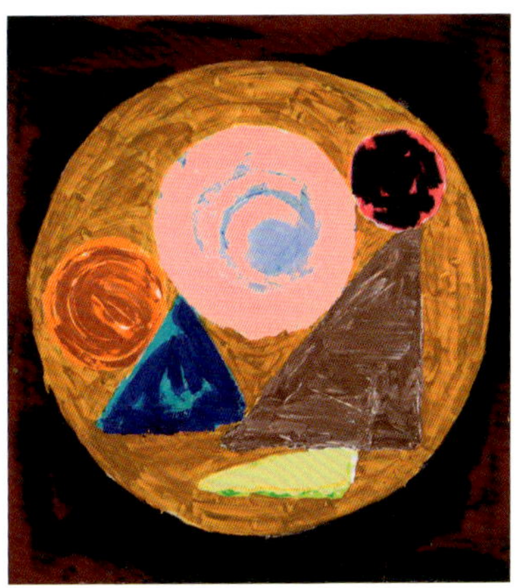

John Hoyland, *Somewhere Before 14.4.84*, 1984
Acrylic on canvas, 244 × 229 cm

Fig.3
Fig.4

control and nailed-down certainty that permeates his images, even as they appear to metamorphosise before our eyes. Hoyland wondered whether Picasso would have been a yet greater artist if he had been more sculptor than painter and praised his paintings as 'blueprints for sculpture…they are so soundly constructed…almost a sculptural concept'.[26] The circle paintings continue Picasso's frequent use of circular or oval forms, which John Golding linked to the foundational modernist ideal of '*le tableau object*', the notion of 'paintings themselves being seen as objects rather than traditional works of art'.[27] The circle paintings were the source for a number of unique platters and plates Hoyland painted in the mid-1980s, although the ease of the move from circular painting motif to circular plate seems to have softened the power of his imagery, keeping it within the decorative or functional, however attractive individual examples are. A wonderful exception is a completely non-functional off-circular ceramic wall piece, made in Umbria at a commune owned by Franciscan monks, which seems to bow with the pressure of the marks placed upon it (p.26).[28]

In the months that Hoyland was making his ceramic sculptures, the Tate Gallery held the major exhibition *Picasso: Sculptor/Painter*.[29] Its impact can be felt in the ceramics. The dotted decoration of Picasso's *Glass of Absinthe* (1914) is relevant, as is the crown of *The Jester* (1905). But Hoyland seems to have been most drawn to the metamorphic sculptures of around

19

1930, traces of which can be found in some of his ceramics. The rotating shapes of Hoyland's *The World* (p.46) rearrange the mutated forms of *Head of Woman* (1931, fig.5). The conical supports, spiralling structure and half-plant, half-person identity of *Imaginary Being* relates to *Bather*[30] (1931). The over-sized feet and ludicrously purposeful stride of *Ruler* recalls Picasso's *Metamorphosis I* (1928). We are far away from Hoyland's High Modernist paintings, especially those of the late 1970s, where Picasso's example primarily existed as a formal framework, a Cubist scaffolding viewed through the images of Nicolas de Staël and Hans Hofmann. At a time when the High Modernist consensus had more or less collapsed, Picasso offered Hoyland a broader vision of Modernism, a sense of risk and of danger, and an art that gained its power from crossing boundaries, rather than tightly mapping them.

It is notable how much the qualities of Hoyland's ceramic sculptures overlap with the new sculptural attitudes that had developed since the early 1980s, in Britain and elsewhere, that were also seeking broader ideas of art, and embraced 'the exuberant use of colour in sculpture…a certain theatricality and a return to recognisable forms, but not to naturalism'.[31] Nena Dimitrijevic saw these wider developments in 'image-based sculpture' as stemming from a return to the irrational and the subconscious, embracing 'symbolism and archetypes':

> *The imperative of stripping bare all the components of art, from material and working processes to its social context, has been replaced by the principle of transfiguration. […] The new sculpture is defined best by the notion of metamorphosis: it is at once materiality and illusion, presence and absence, sculpture and its double-image, caught up into an inseparable unity.*[32]

The third and final phase of Hoyland's paintings of the 1980s were the epic sky-writing paintings of 1988–91. The circle paintings seem as much carved as painted, hewn with some difficulty out of great blocks of pigment. Looking to Miró more than Picasso, the sky-writing paintings inject a burst of energy, their looping calligraphies moving Hoyland's art back into the realm of the visual. Their interlacing lines can be traced to the tendrils of paintings such as *25.6.66* (1966, fig.2), and perhaps beyond those to the Chinese-vase-inspired paintings of 1962–63, and in turn provide the structure for the most complex of the ceramics, *Thupelo Memory*, *The Wheel* (p.51), *Warrior* and *Roots*.

The sky-writing paintings were the result of a complex movement between two and three dimensions in a more direct sense. Many began with arrangements of string laid on the paint-splattered floor of Hoyland's studio, seemingly mixing chance and deliberation, then recorded in Polaroid photographs (see pp.114–123). These small photographic images are followed with surprising accuracy, if completely transformed effect, in the lassoing motifs of the succeeding paintings. Many are more than two metres tall and they demonstrate Hoyland's great facility as a manipulator of paint in motion. The movement from string to Polaroid to painting and then into the ropes of the ceramics shows the importance to his imagination of an interplay between two and three dimensions.

An upright monolithic form floats in the centre of some of the sky-writing paintings, a condensed sculptural image launched in a non-sculptural environment, most dramatically in *Siren 10.7.89* (1989, fig.6). The staging of such a shape against a visual and seemingly infinite backdrop links these paintings back to his upright verticals of around 1970, which often contained thickly painted motifs positioned against stained fields of colour. These were perhaps partly inspired by his establishing a studio in 1968 near the Neolithic standing stones of Avebury. A heterogenous

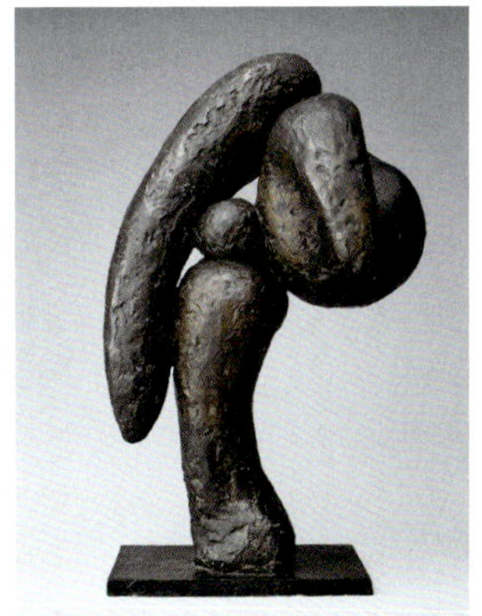

Pablo Picasso, *Head of Woman*
(Tête de femme), 1931
Bronze, 71.5 × 41 × 33 cm
Musée National Picasso, Paris

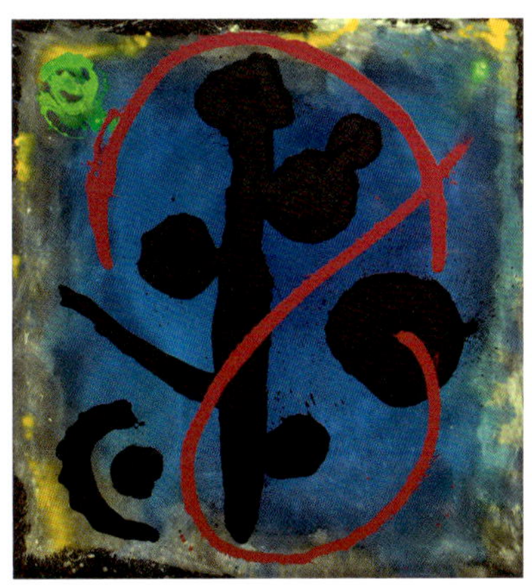

John Hoyland, *Siren 10.7.89*, 1989
Acrylic on canvas, 254 × 236 cm

Fig.5
Fig.6

list Hoyland composed of his influences juxtaposed 'masks, mirrors, Avebury Circle, views from planes'.[33] Attenuated verticals, echoes of monoliths, can be found occasionally in his paintings until his death in 2011; images of the individual against the cosmos.

The ceramics summarise and mark the end of Hoyland's paintings of the dozen years between 1982 and 1994, even if his work resists such neat compartmentalisation. Shortly after making them Hoyland embarked on his Bali paintings, inspired by his visits to the Indonesian island, initiating a new period in his art. He had been taking Polaroid photographs of his travels since the 1980s (see pp.114–123), as part of his opening up to the world, his search for 'new hybrids'. But with the Bali paintings these found motifs became much more overtly present in the final paintings. They became populated by Balinese pennants, vegetation and bird-scarers. Motifs from Bali were later joined by those drawn from Cuba, Jamaica, Puerto Rico and other Caribbean islands, forming a broader group of what could be called the 'voyage paintings', dramatic and fantastical images of a visionary semi-figuration, where natural and man-made motifs weave in and out of vibrant fields of colour. The voyage paintings continued to around the millennium, shortly after which his paintings began a final emptying-out, into cosmic voids that ruminated on his increasing consciousness of mortality.[34] On the cusp between these two broad final phases of his work are

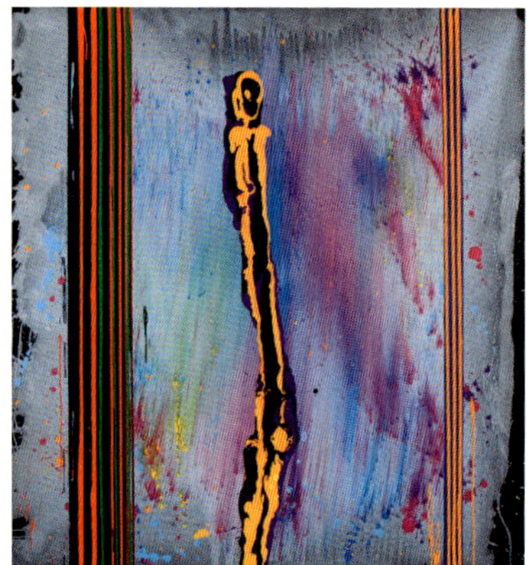

John Hoyland, *River Man 15.7.99*, 1999
Acrylic on canvas, 254 × 236 cm

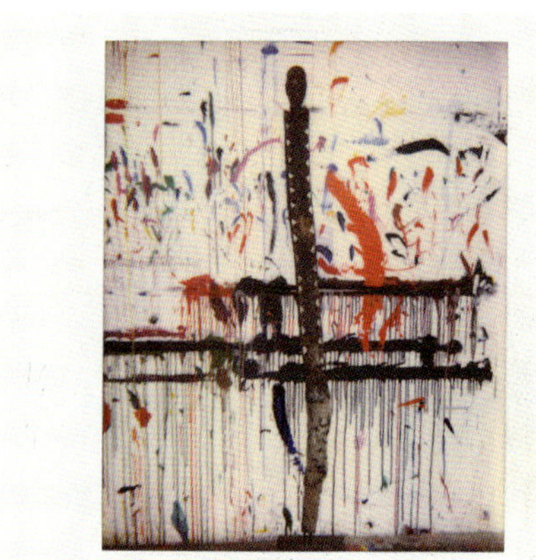

Polaroid photograph taken by
John Hoyland, undated

Fig.7
Fig.8

paintings that originated in a last engagement with sculpture. *River Man 15.7.99* (1999, fig.7), *Alone 21.10.00* and *The Abyss 7.11.00* (both 2000) are among those in which Hoyland explored motifs based on an 'African grave sculpture' from his collection.[35] He positioned its thin, slanted figure against his studio wall, or in dialogue with already completed paintings, recording the results in a series of Polaroid photographs (fig.8), although the final paintings completely belie the photographic aspects of their making.[36] In these startling paintings the African sculpture is removed from its original meaning and context. It becomes an emblem of identification with the world outside of Europe and stands as a tragic everyman, isolated within the intensity, immensity and shuddering beauty of the universe.

1   Kathleen Hoyland, letter to John Hoyland, 9 September 1977, The John Hoyland Archive. This letter states that Hoyland made these early ceramics while at the 'junior art school', that is, the Sheffield School of Arts & Crafts (Junior Department), meaning he would have been at least 11 years old, rather than 7, as he claimed in the pamphlet for the CCA exhibition: *John Hoyland: Ceramic Works, 1994*, CCA Galleries, London, 1–25 June 1994 (see fig.1, p.14 of this book). Glitter wax was a modelling wax manufactured by the Cosmic Crayon Company, Bedford. *Official Gazette of the United States Patent Office*, 5 August 1924, p.18.

2   Mike von Joel, 'Hoyland at Home', *Art Line*, no.4, February 1983, p.11.

3   Hoyland included the date of completion in the titles of his paintings. In his Notebook EII, page 104, he simply recorded '25 ceramics', between *Mirror People 23.12.93* (1993) and *Trance 6.6.94* (1994). The John Hoyland Archive.

4   'In the winter of 1962–63, visiting the artist's studio, I saw an illustration of a Chinese vase or lamp pinned up on a wall which was evidently a source of the paintings concerned with a sinuously moving band of colour, like a river, later to be complicated with additional bands'. Bryan Robertson, 'Introduction', in *John Hoyland: Paintings 1960–67*, exhibition catalogue, Whitechapel Gallery, London, 1967, p.11.

5   Miró, 1941–42, quoted in Laura Coyle, 'The Monsters in America: The Presentation and Reception of Miró's Sculpture in the United States', *The Shape of Color: Joan Miró: Painted Sculpture*, exhibition catalogue, Corcoran Gallery of Art, Washington, DC, 2002, p.67.

6   'John Hoyland Interviewed by Mel Gooding', *National Life Story Collection: Artists' Lives*, p.147. Transcript in The John Hoyland Archive.

7   'Listings', *RA Magazine*, no.43, summer 1994, p.83.

8   Howard Jacobson, 'The Colourful Life of John Hoyland', *Arts & Books Review*, *The Independent*, 28 April 2006, p.2.

9   Philip Dodd, 'Introduction', in *The Doors of Perception: The Art of John Hoyland*, exhibition catalogue, Daugavpils Mark Rothko Art Centre, Daugavpils, 2023, n.p.

10   'Listings', *op. cit.*, p.83.

11   'I may be an artist, but I'm not a connoisseur. I'm interested in an object as a form that I like, something nourishing to look at which, I hope, in some way or other will filter in and enrich my own work'. Hoyland quoted in Richard Barber, 'Artist in Residence', *Homes and Antiques*, August 1999, p.35.

12   Hoyland bought the sculpture in a warehouse in Sydney. *Ibid.*, p.38.

13   'What I hope to do is to make cross-cultural hybrids. I'd love to make paintings that could cross social, linguistic and cultural barriers in the way that music does. It's a dream, but an enjoyable one. It may be doomed – like Esperanto! I don't accept the dominance of European culture, or the centrality of the Renaissance. From my point of view, the world is open, culturally speaking'. Bryan Robertson, 'John Hoyland', *Modern Painters*, vol.7, no.1, Spring 1994, p.34.

14   Guillem Ramos-Poquí, letter to John Hoyland, 7 June 1994. The John Hoyland Archive.

15   Hambling was originally asked to decorate plates or bowls, but decided she wanted to make independent sculptures. Author interview with Maggi Hambling, 21 April 2023. The project was perhaps initiated by potter Janice Tchalenko (1942–2018), who taught at the RCA in the 1980s and 1990s. Email from David Hamilton to the author 9 January 2023.

16   'The paintings of the late Eighties were dominated by a roughly centralised calligraphic arabesque, a magisterial signature, as if sky-written against the immensities of celestial space'. Mel Gooding, 'The Dialectics of Vision: Hoyland's Bali Paintings', in *John Hoyland: Bali Paintings*, exhibition catalogue, Theo Waddington Fine Art, London, 1995, n.p.

17   'John Hoyland Interviewed by Mel Gooding', *op. cit.*, p.194.

18   *Ibid*.

19   These six are reproduced in the CCA pamphlet for *John Hoyland: Ceramic Works, 1994*, *op. cit.* and a copy of the price list is in The John Hoyland Archive.

20   Robertson, *John Hoyland: Paintings 1960–67*, *op. cit.*, pp.3–4.

21   Robert Melville and Bryan Robertson, 'Introduction', in *The English Eye*, exhibition catalogue, Marlborough-Gerson Gallery, New York, 1965, p.12.

22   *25.6.66* was one of a group of paintings likened to 'coloured Plasticine […] hanging heavy with succulence'. M.G McNay, 'Alan Davie at the Queen Square Gallery, Leeds and Six Artists at the Mappin Gallery, Sheffield', *The Guardian*, 2 July 1996; the phrase 'dream-space' occurs in 'John Hoyland Interviewed by Mel Gooding', *op. cit.*, p.123.

23   Robertson, 'John Hoyland', *op. cit.*, p.34.

24   Mel Gooding, *John Hoyland*, Thames & Hudson, London, 2006, p.125.

25   *Ibid.*, p.130.

26   'I've often thought with Picasso that he might have been an even greater artist if, instead of a third of his work being sculpture and the other two thirds painting, it had been the other way round. Because his paintings are like blueprints for sculpture, they are so soundly constructed with the planes and the proportions and the dynamics of them. This is almost a sculptural concept. You can't have power without structure'. Martin Gayford, 'John Hoyland on Pablo Picasso's Seated Musketeer with Sword (1969)', *The Daily Telegraph*, 18 August 2001.

27   John Golding, 'Introduction', in Elizabeth Cowling and John Golding (eds), *Picasso: Sculptor/Painter*, exhibition catalogue, Tate Gallery, London, 1994, p.22.

28   Barber, 'Artist in Residence', *op. cit.*, p.37.

29   *Picasso: Sculptor/Painter* ran from 16 February to 8 May 1994.

30   Pablo Picasso, *Baigneuse* (*Bather*), 1931, Musée National Picasso, Paris (inv. MP289).

31   Nena Dimitrijevic, 'Sculpture and its Double: Towards a Definition of Post-evolutionary Sculpture', in *The Sculpture Show*, exhibition catalogue, Hayward Gallery and Serpentine Gallery, London, 1983, p.138.

32   *Ibid.*, p.142.

33   This list exists in different versions. The one quoted here is from the manuscript of a talk given at the Tate in 1994, 'Invisible Artist or Performing Bear'. The John Hoyland Archive.

34   Natalie Adamson, David Anfam, Matthew Collings and Mel Gooding, *John Hoyland: The Last Paintings*, Ridinghouse, London, 2021.

35   As described by Hoyland in Virgina Boston, 'Getting Metaphysical: John Hoyland Interviewed', *Artists & Illustrators*, July 2000, p.33. He purchased the sculpture from the General Trading Company, Sloane Street, London. See Barber, 'Artist in Residence', *op. cit.*, p.38.

36   In *Waterman 9.11.00* (2000) the African sculpture's head and shoulders float next to a circular, biomorphic motif that is almost certainly based upon the bowed ceramic platter Hoyland made in Umbria. Other of Hoyland's Polaroids employ an African mask and the New Guinea bird sculpture in a similar manner.

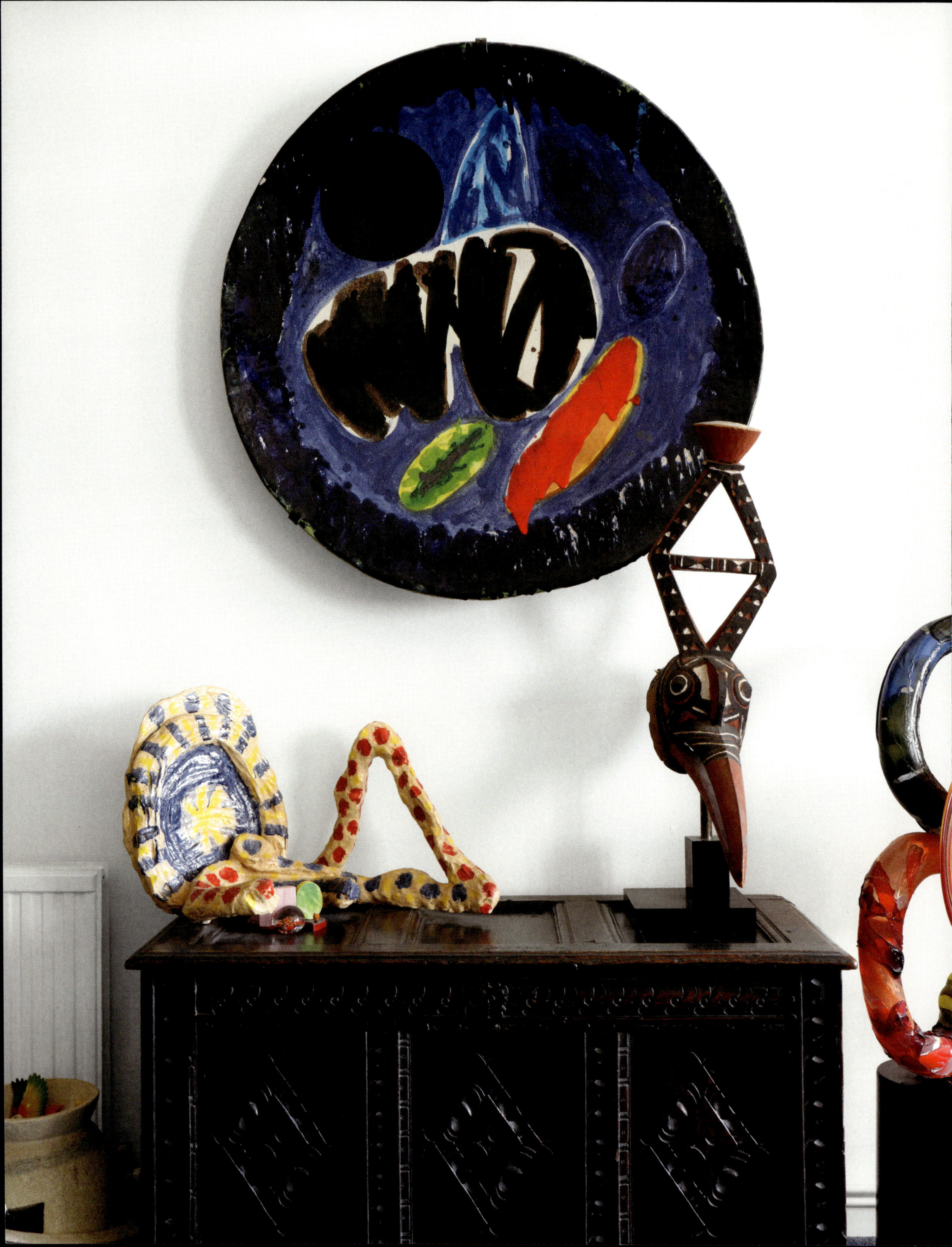

Ceramics

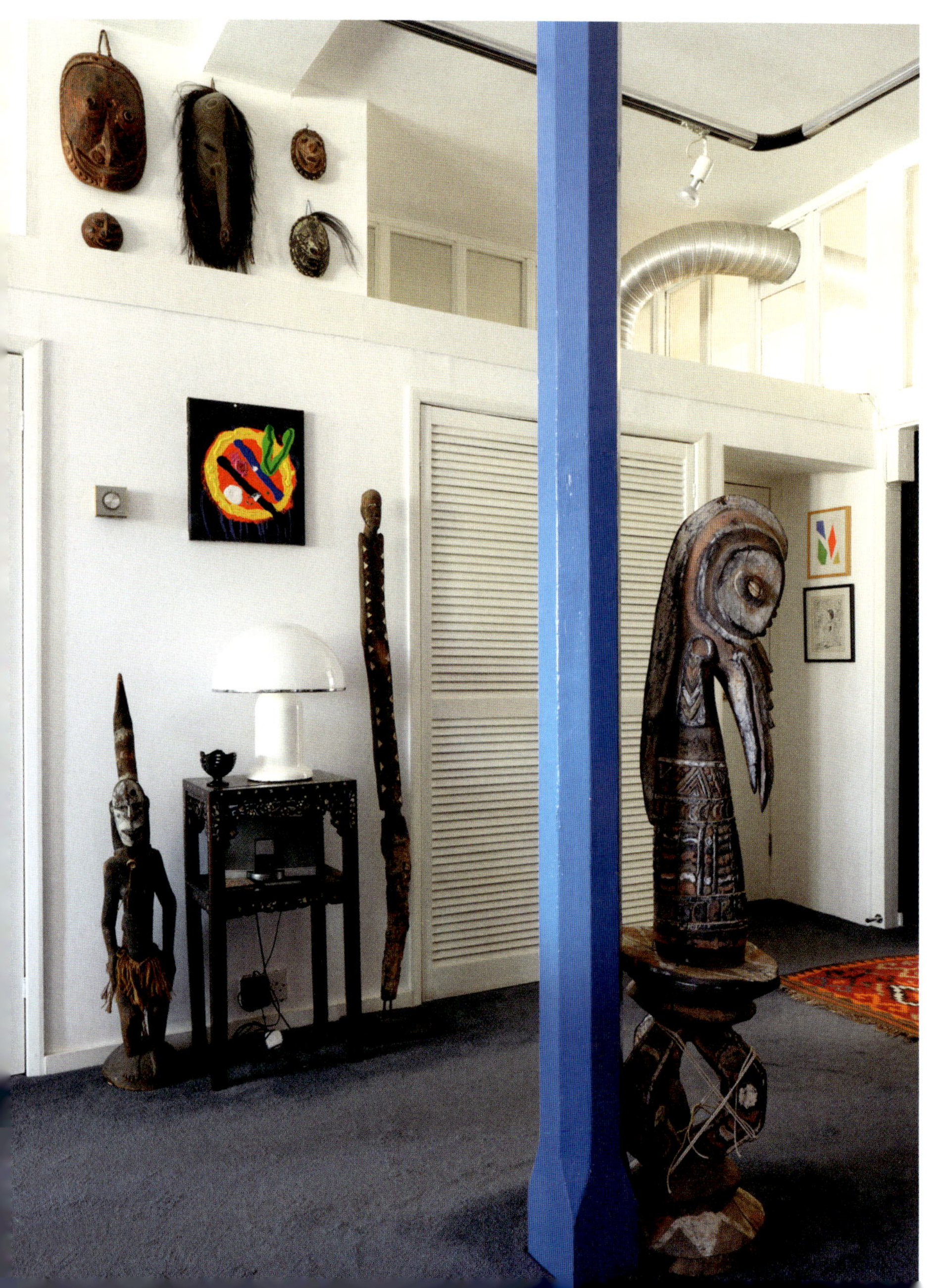

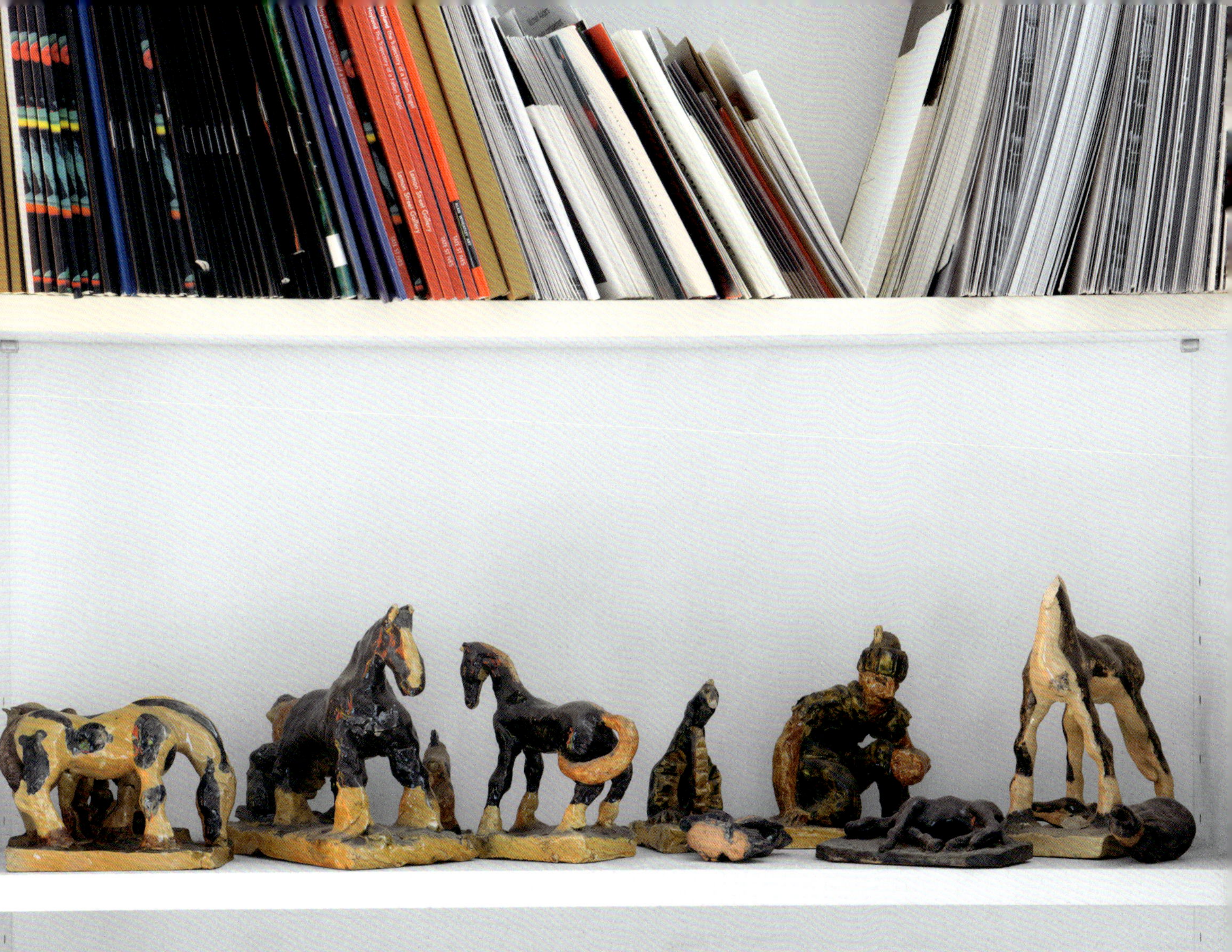

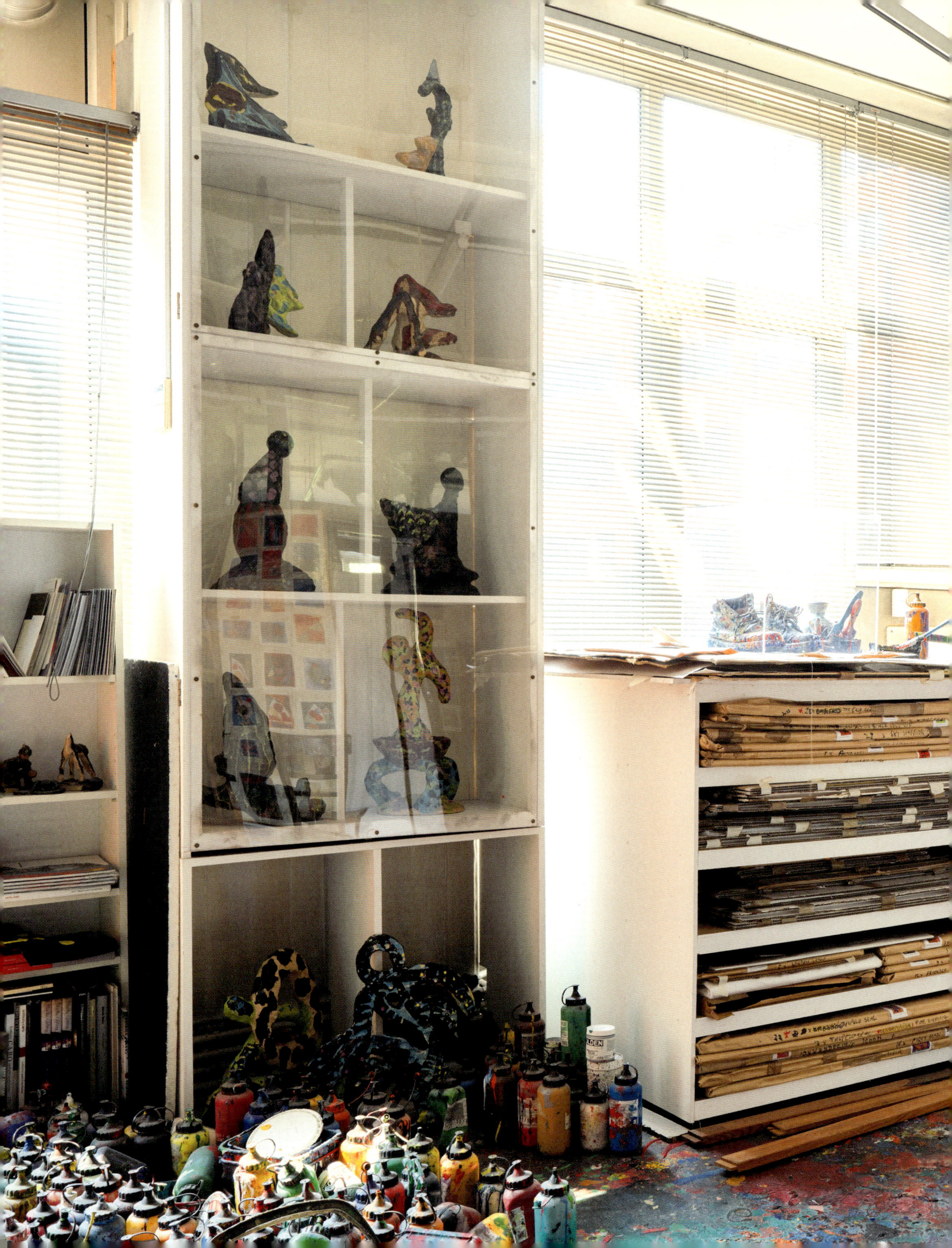

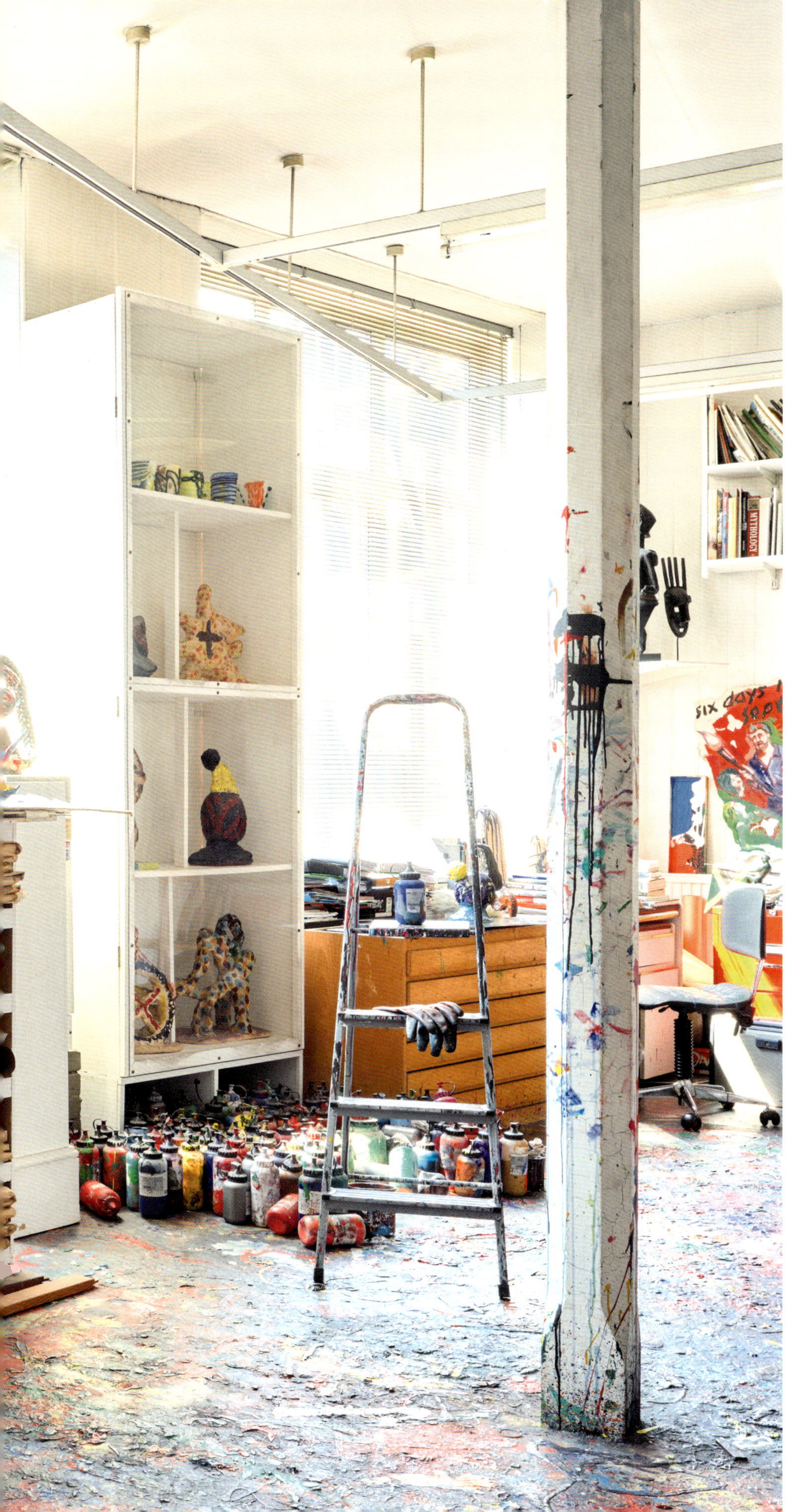

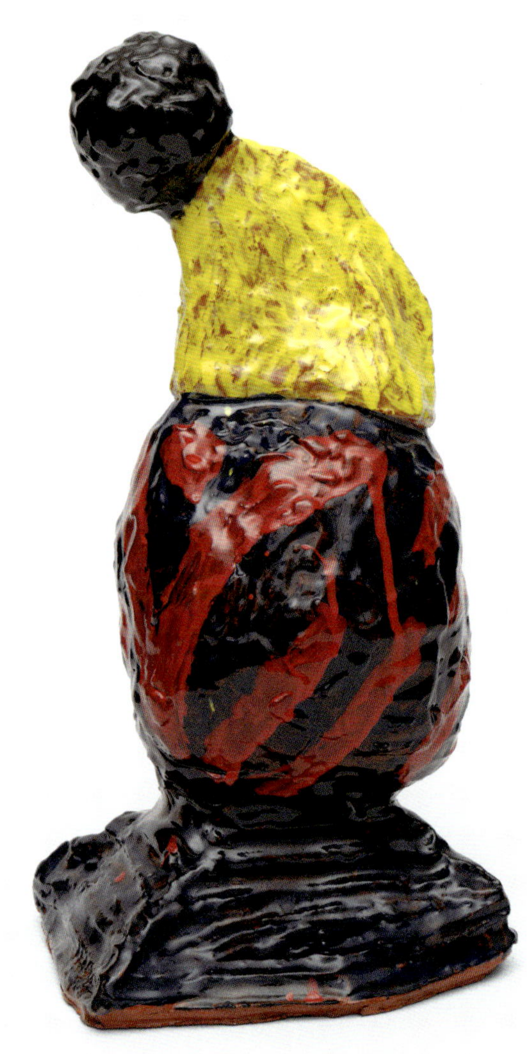

John Hoyland, *Bablaz*, 1994
Glazed ceramic, 40 × 26 × 28 cm

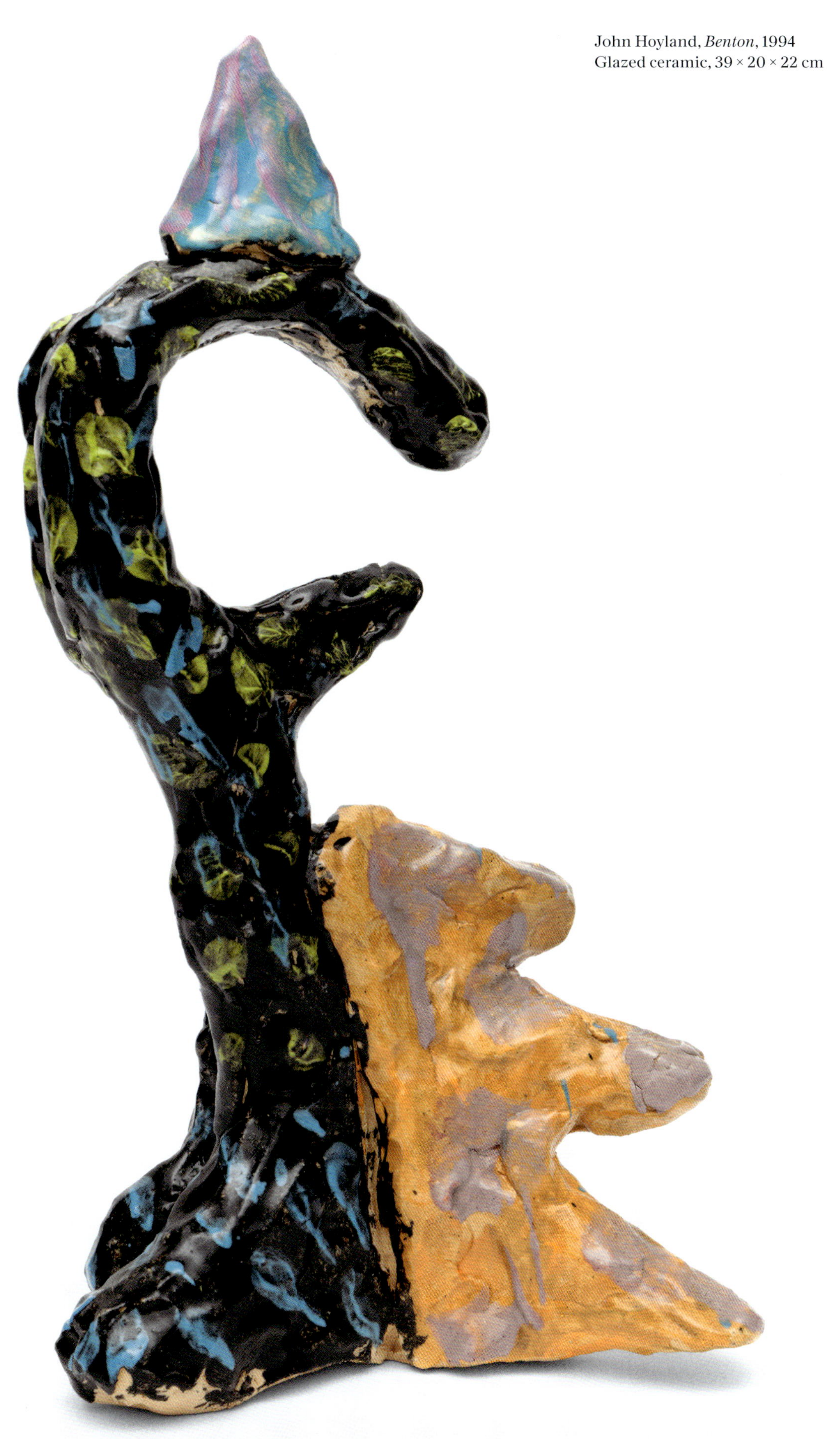

John Hoyland, *Benton*, 1994
Glazed ceramic, 39 × 20 × 22 cm

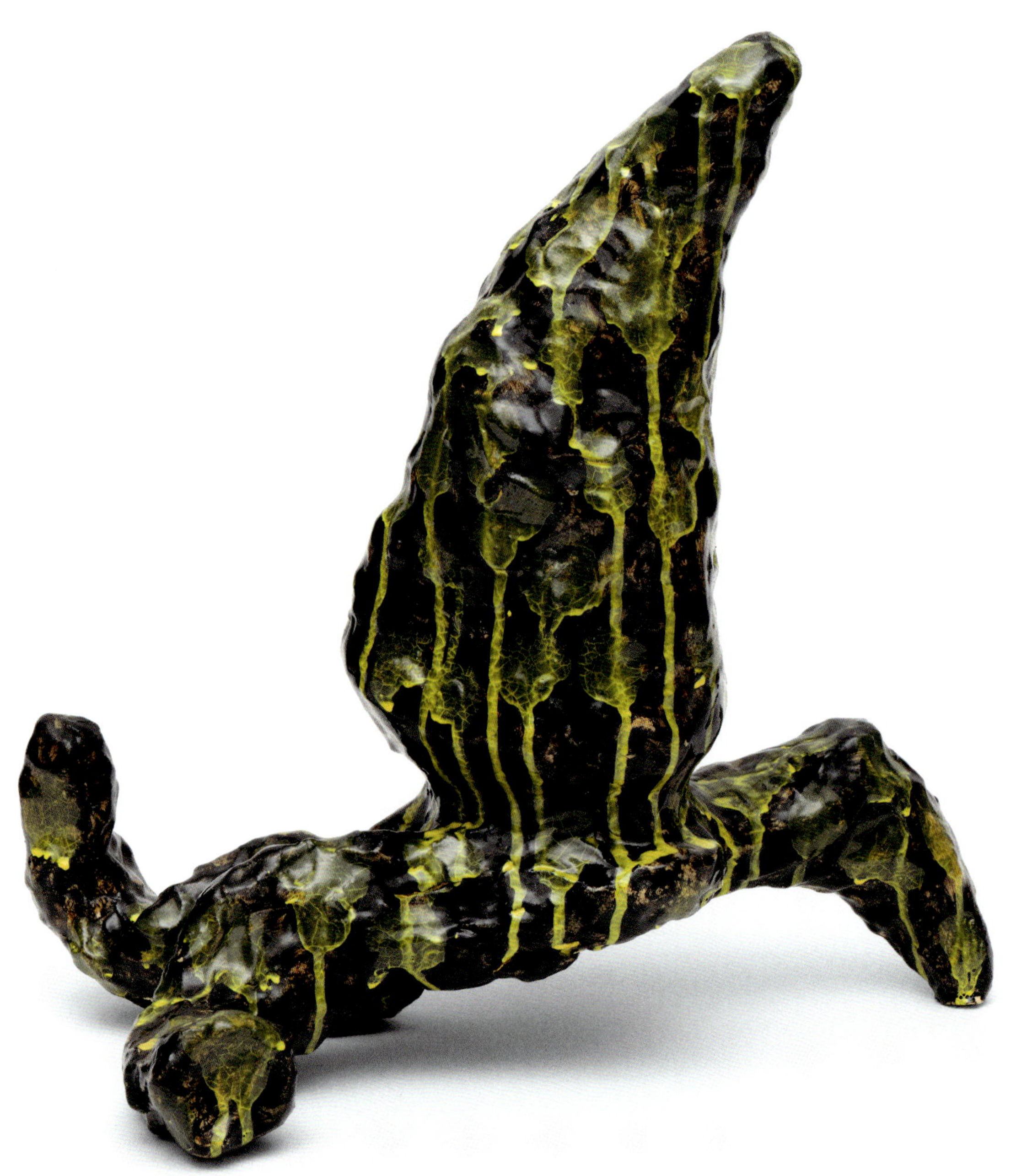

John Hoyland, *Conjuror*, 1994
Glazed ceramic, 41 × 42 × 24 cm

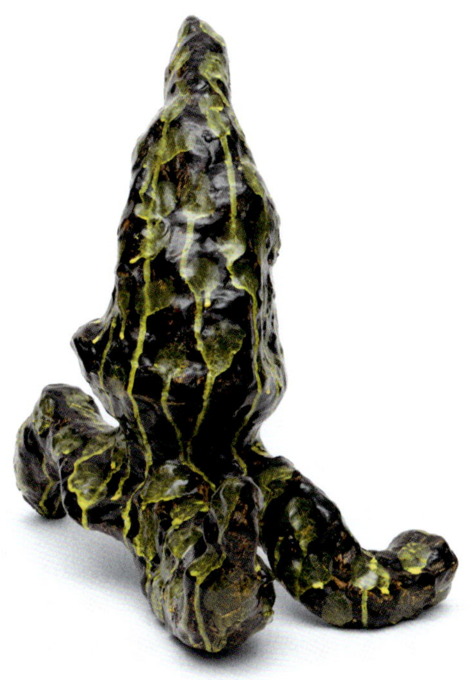

John Hoyland, *Dragon*, 1994
Glazed ceramic, 33 × 25 × 49 cm

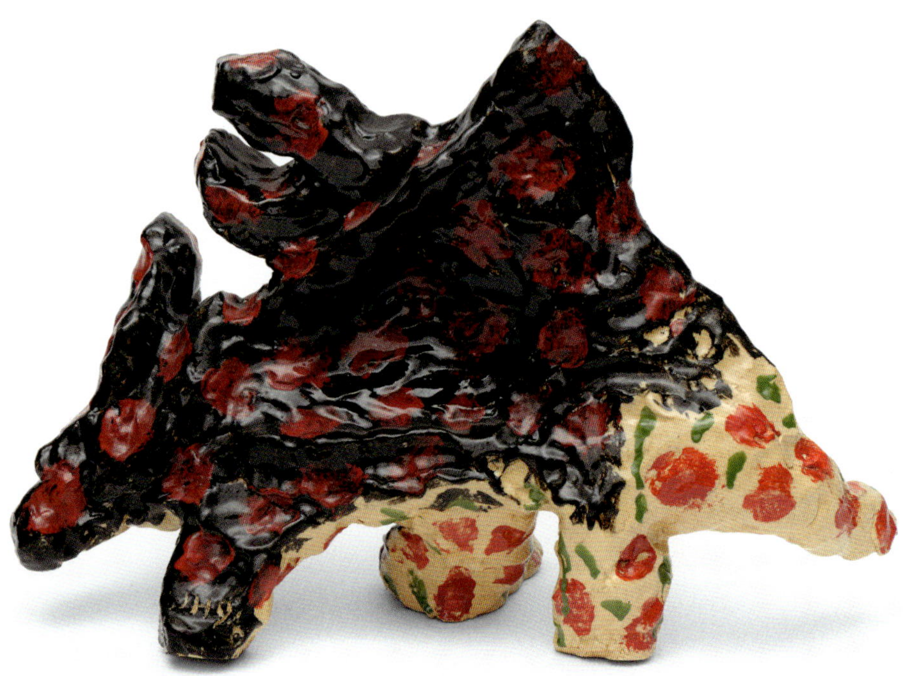

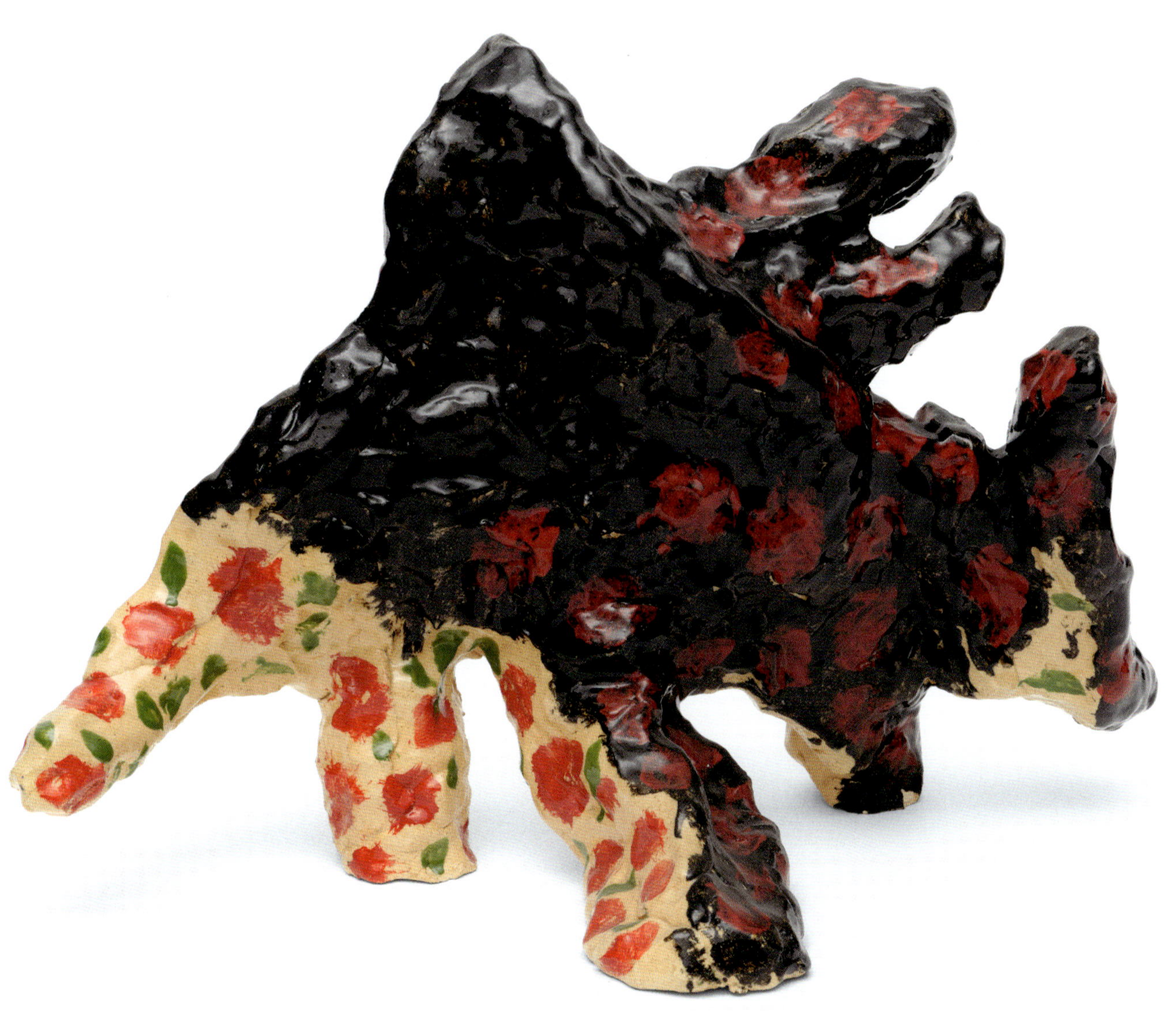

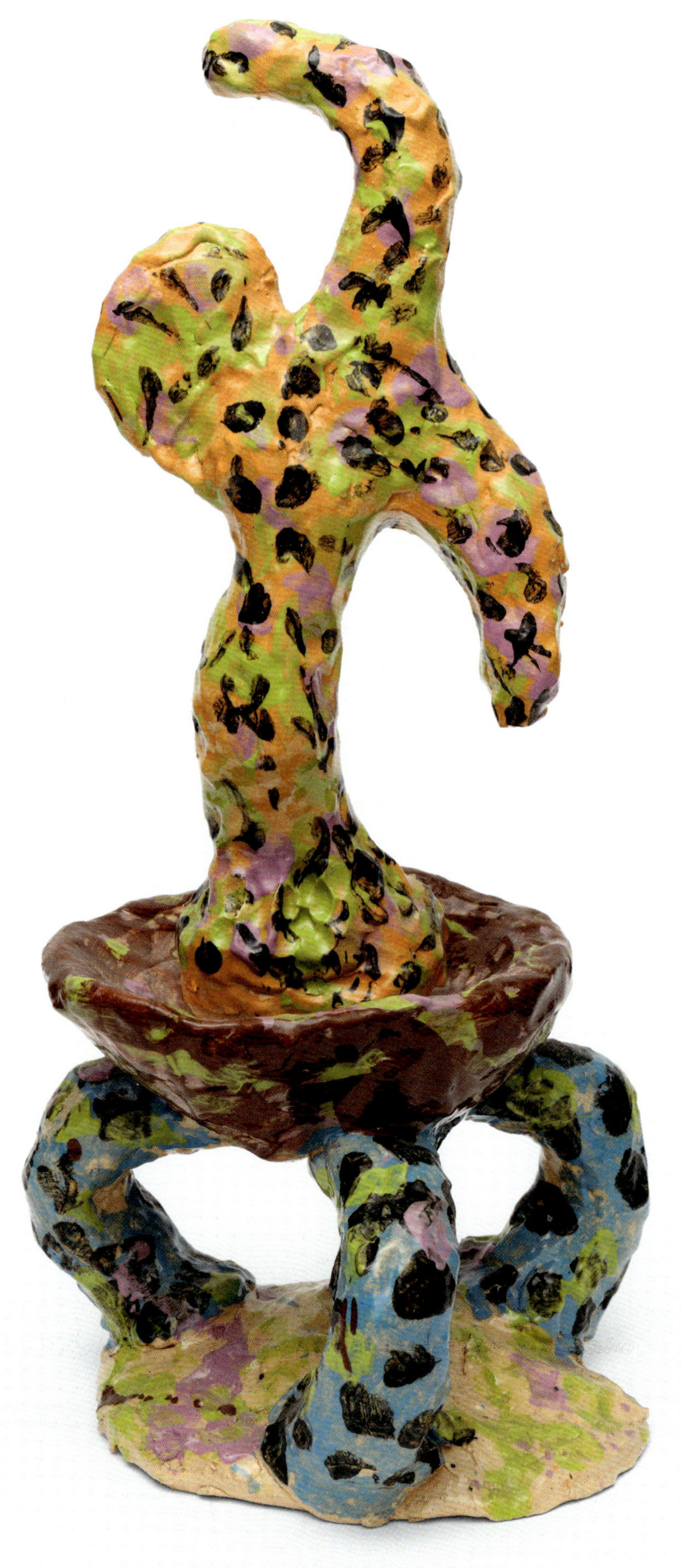

John Hoyland, *Imaginary Being*, 1994
Glazed ceramic, 57 × 24 × 27 cm

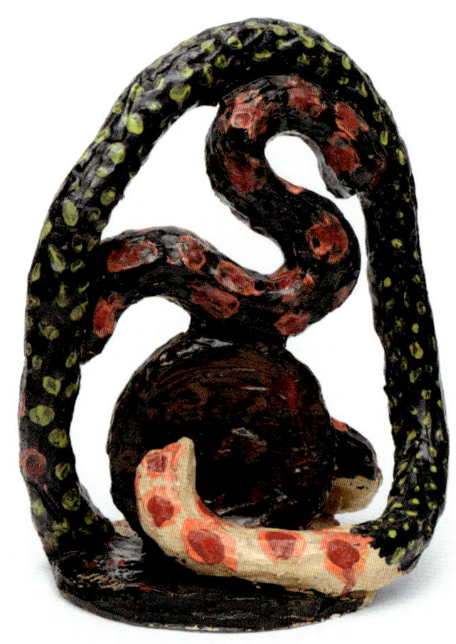

John Hoyland, *Lamia*, 1994
Glazed ceramic, 39 × 33 × 26 cm

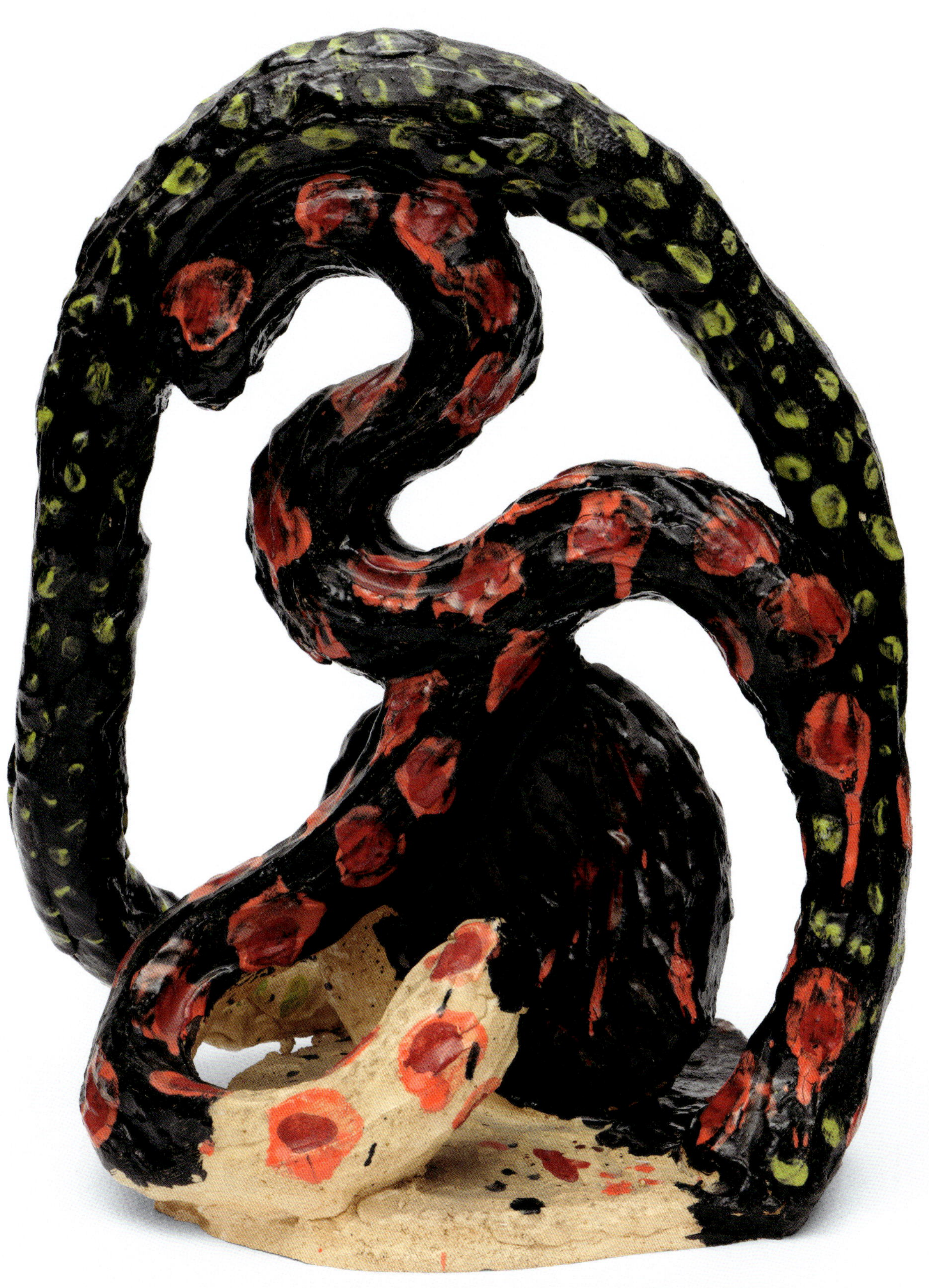

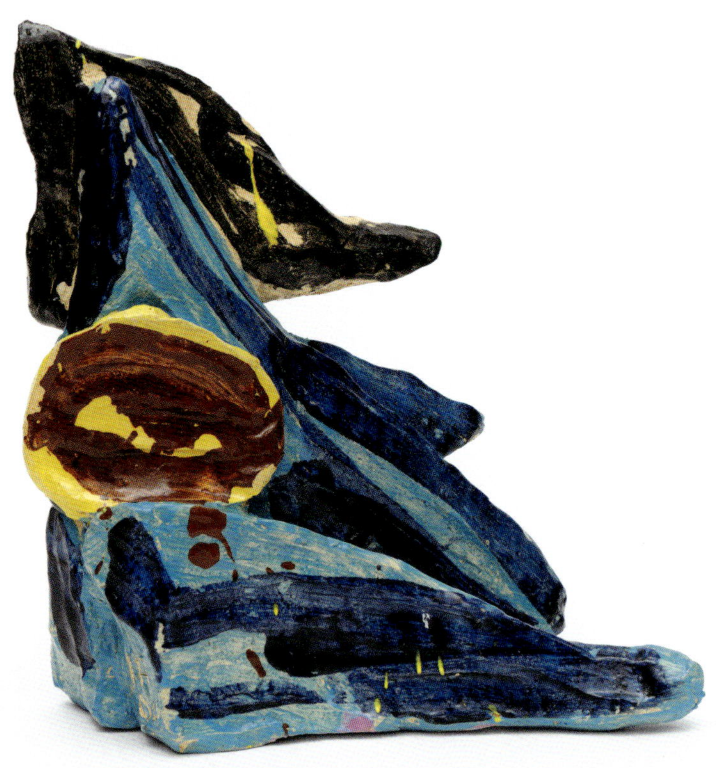

John Hoyland, *Ocean Man*, 1994
Glazed ceramic, 27 × 11 × 26 cm

John Hoyland, *Ruler*, 1994
Glazed ceramic, 38 × 32 × 13 cm

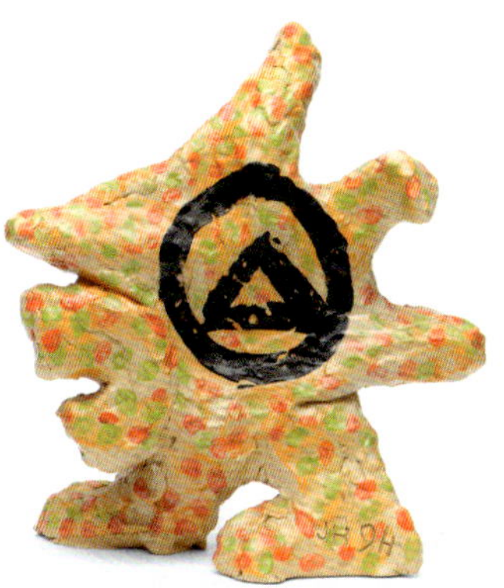

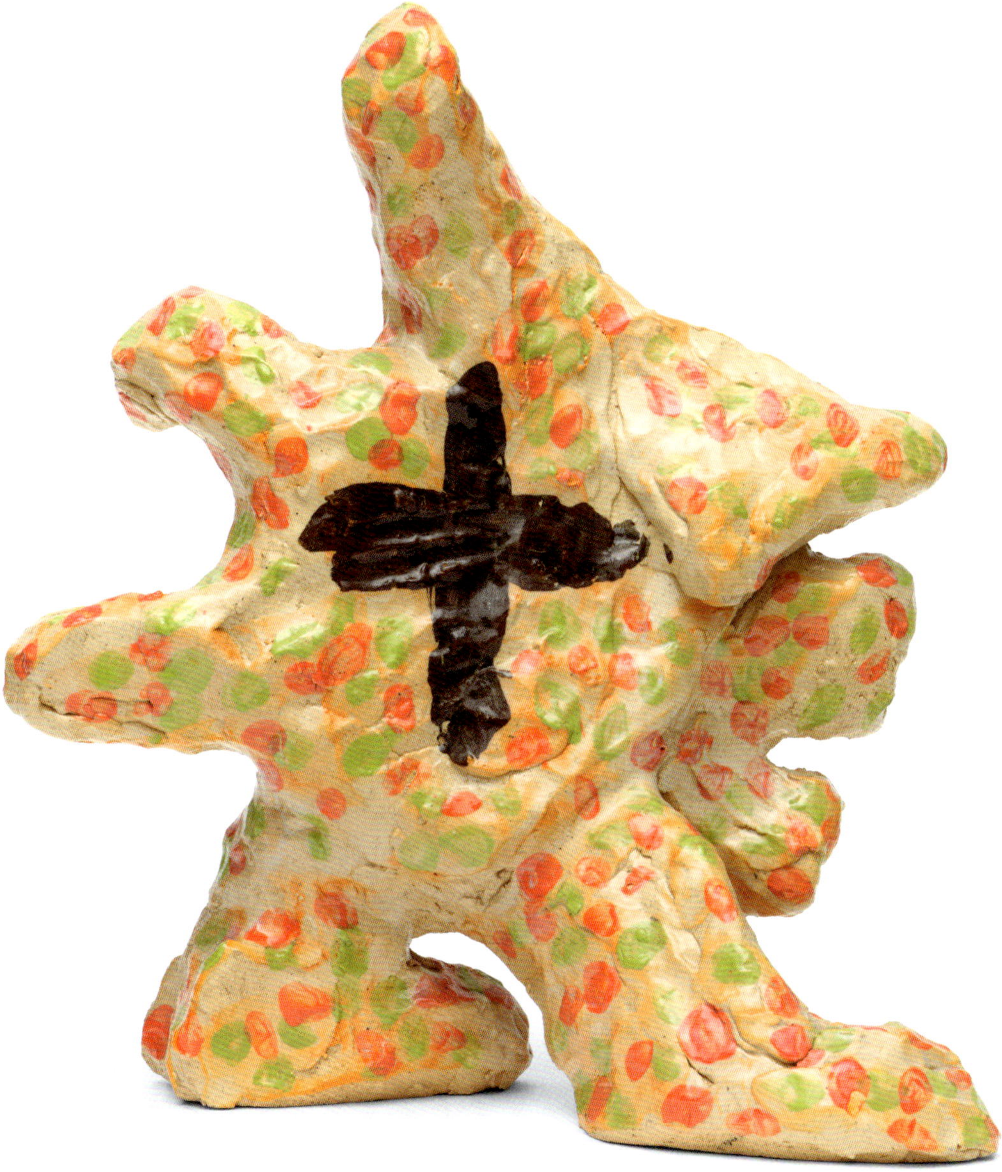

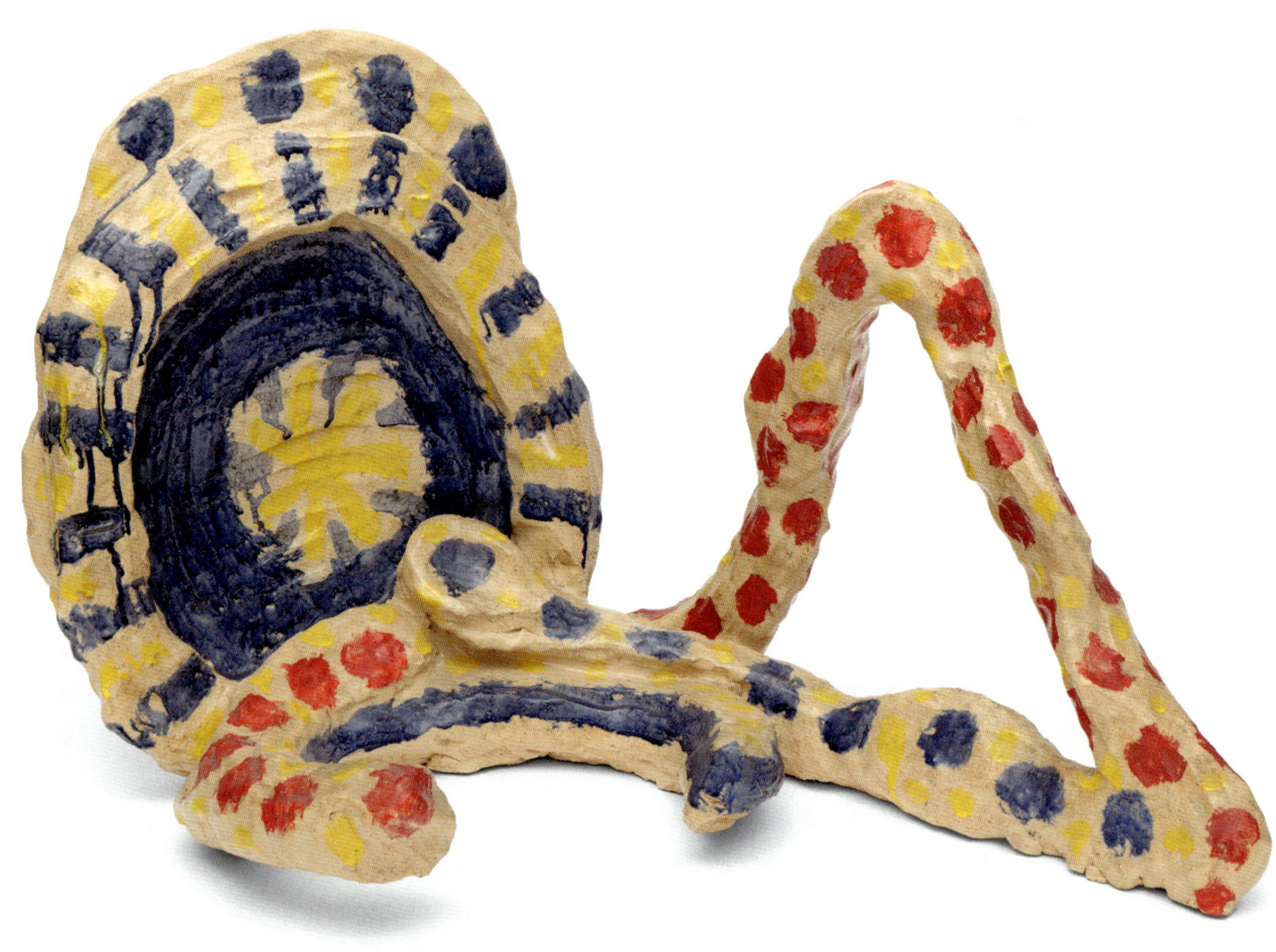

John Hoyland, *The King*, 1994
Glazed ceramic, 66 × 43 × 38 cm

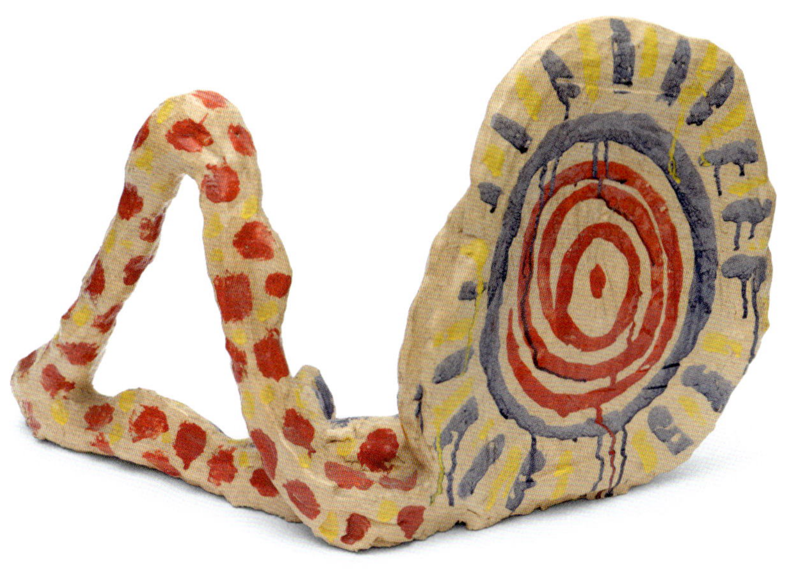

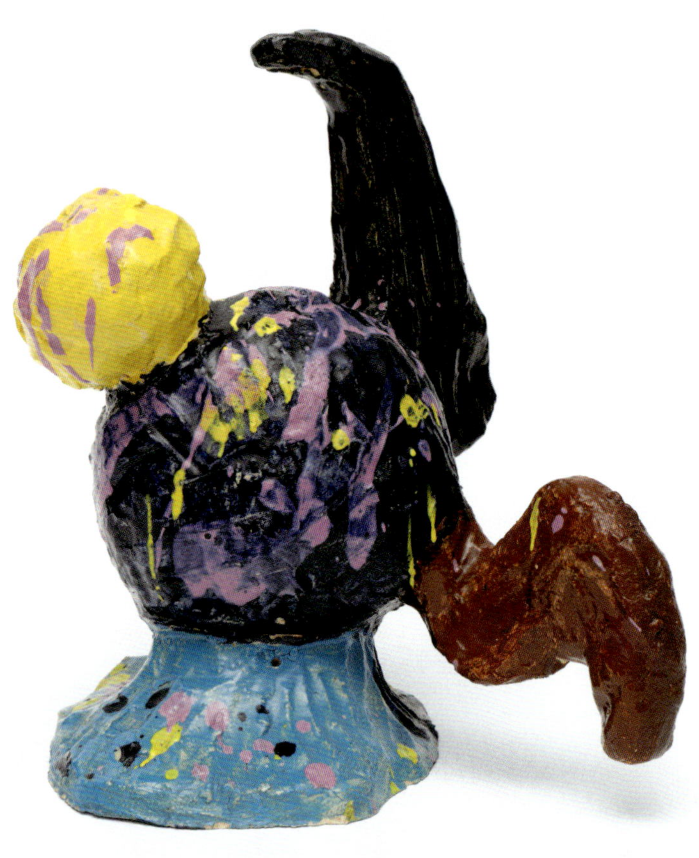

John Hoyland, *The World*, 1994
Glazed ceramic, 29 × 29 × 19 cm

John Hoyland, *Thupelo Memory*, 1994
Glazed ceramic, 36 × 35 × 46 cm

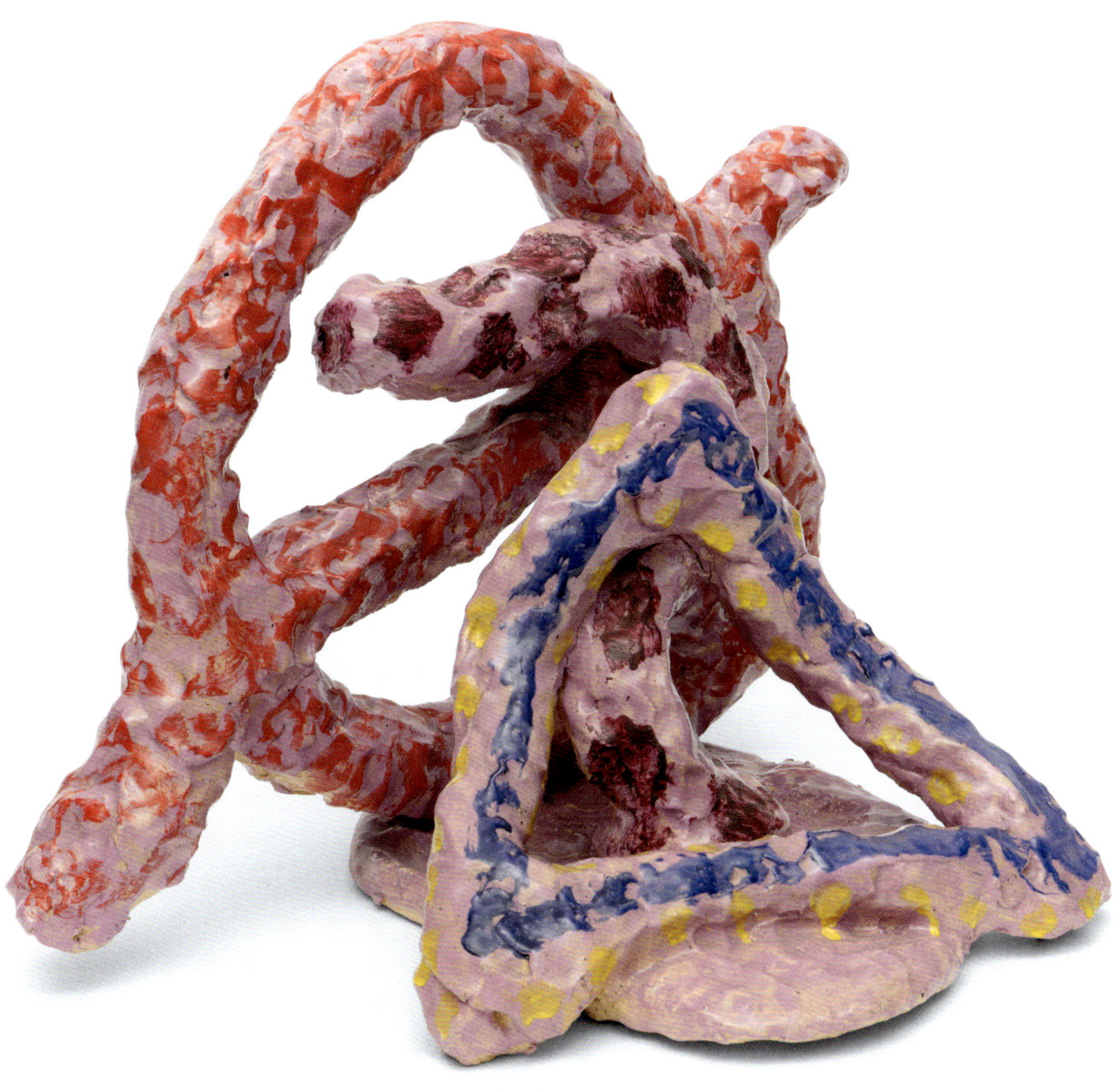

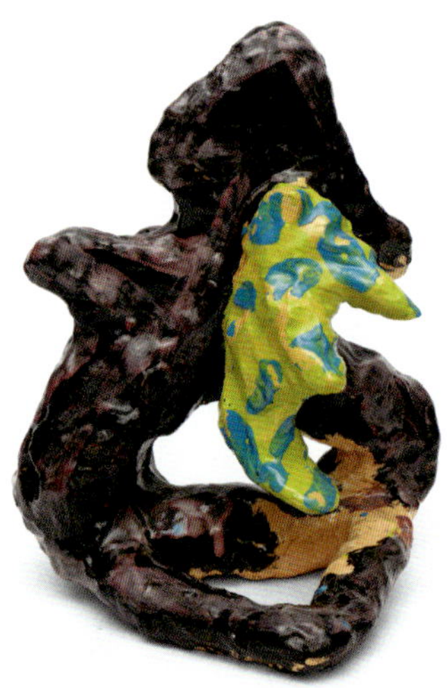

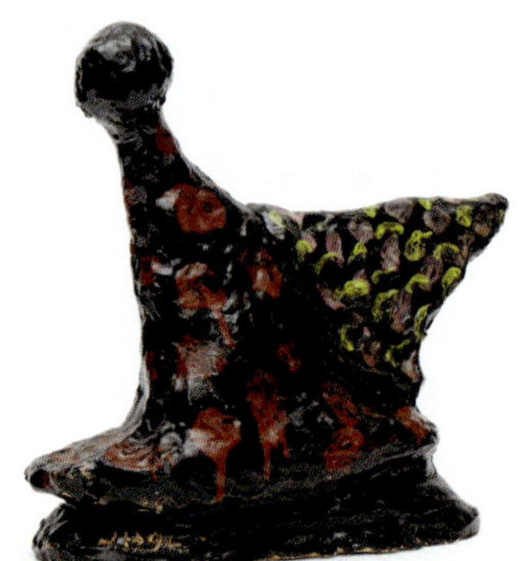

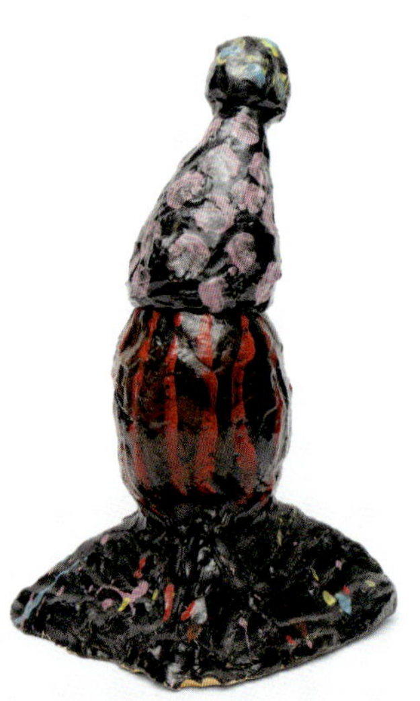

John Hoyland, *Doppie*, 1994
Glazed ceramic, 38 × 40 × 14 cm

John Hoyland, *Animal Imagined*, 1994
Glazed ceramic, 35.6 × 30.5 × 17.8 cm

John Hoyland, *Enigma*, 1994
Glazed ceramic, 41 × 10 × 10 cm

48

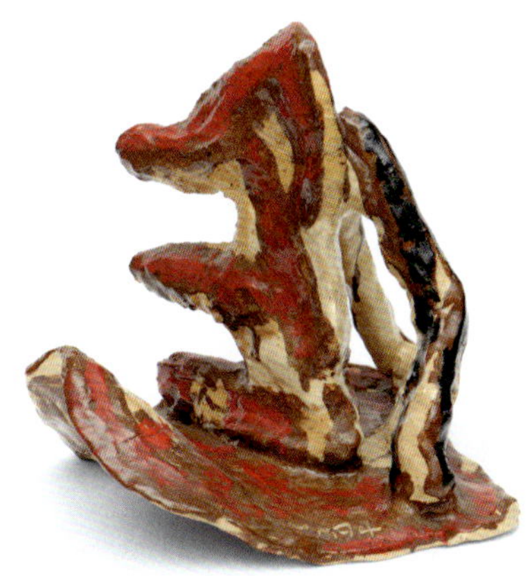

John Hoyland, *Fauna*, 1994
Glazed ceramic, 30 × 33 × 31 cm

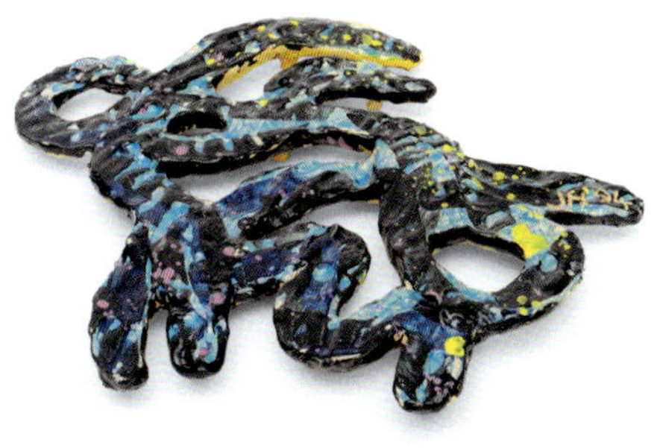

John Hoyland, *First Man*, 1994
Glazed ceramic, 50.8 × 48 × 5 cm

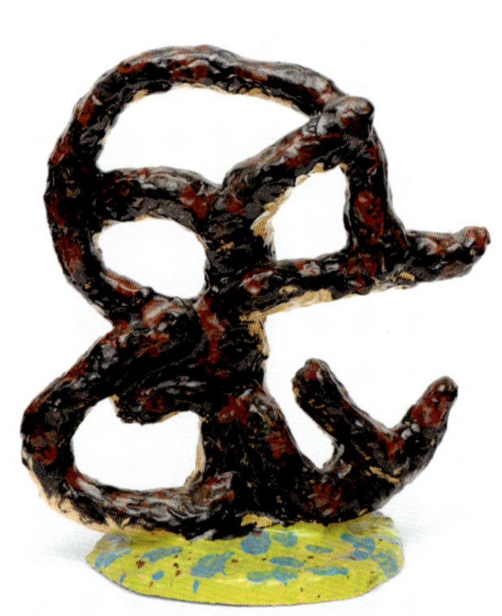

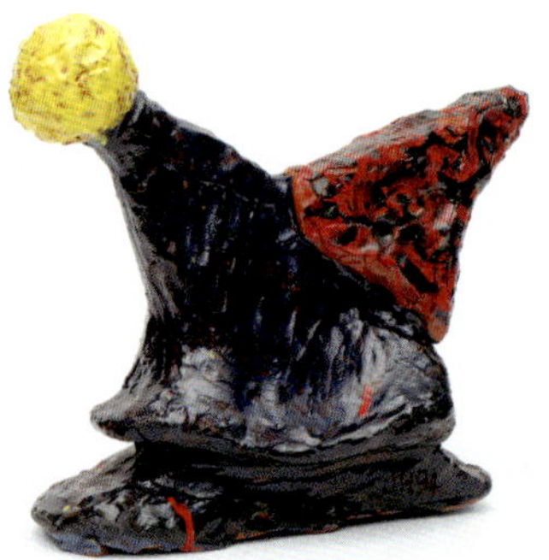

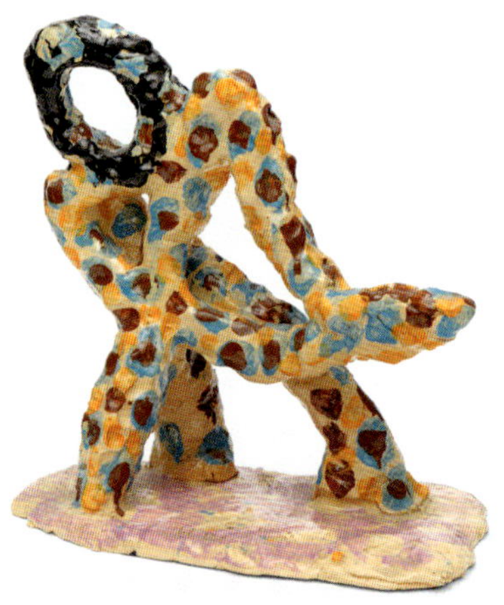

John Hoyland, *Roots*, 1994
Glazed ceramic, 46 × 39 × 28 cm

John Hoyland, *Sorcerer*, 1994
Glazed ceramic, 42 × 45 × 10 cm

John Hoyland, *Sun Animal*, 1994
Glazed ceramic, 29 × 35 × 15 cm

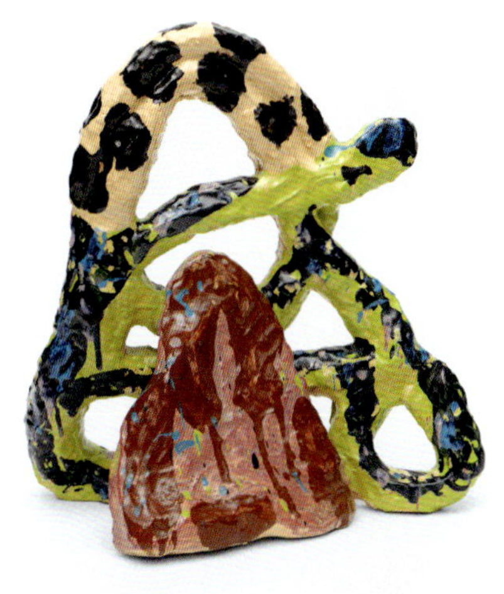

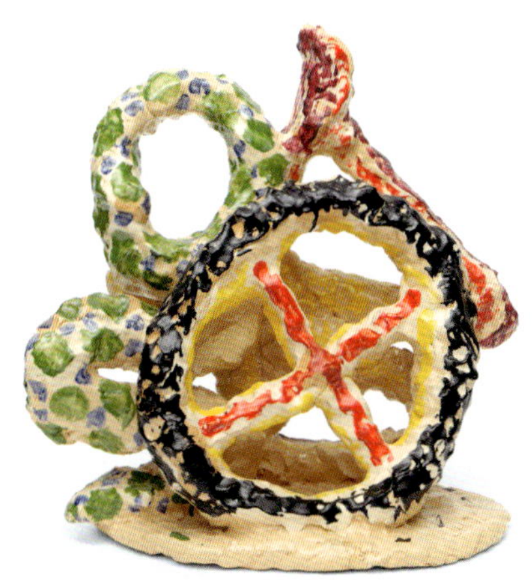

John Hoyland, *The Wheel*, 1994
Glazed ceramic, 43 × 42 × 10 cm

John Hoyland, *Warrior*, 1994
Glazed ceramic, 45 × 42 × 25.4 cm

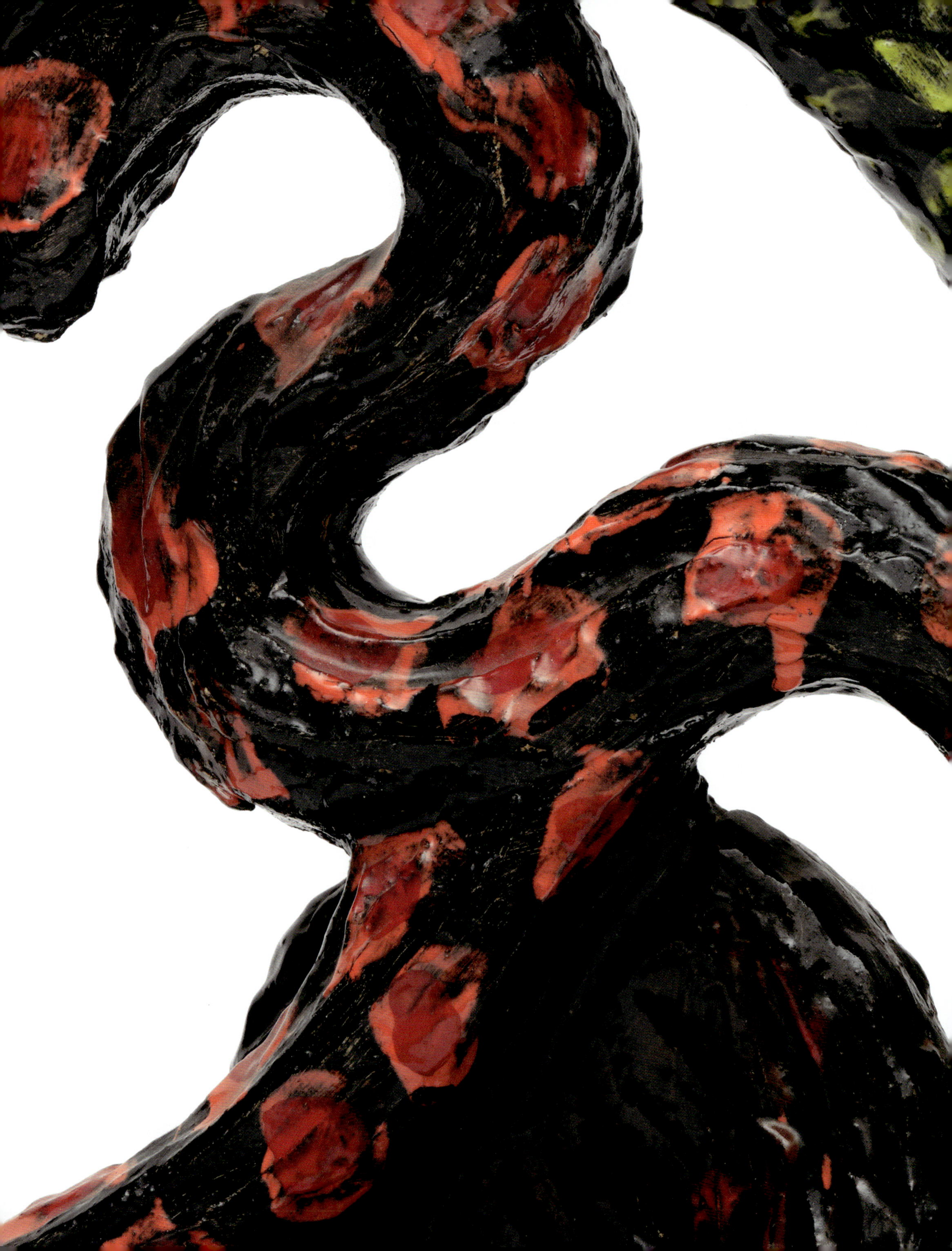

These Mad Hybrids: John Hoyland's Ceramics and Contemporary Sculpture

Olivia Bax

John Hoyland's ceramic sculpture, *Thupelo Memory* (1994, pp.47 and 55), is bubblegum pink. Crudely stamped and scored with other colours – blue, yellow, purple and red – it has been constructed with clay sausages and looks simultaneously linear and solid. The scatological reference is un-missable, with a tired triangle and a perky pretzel sitting atop a cowpat. It perches on a low stool in his apartment which affirms the visual meta-phor. Next door, in Hoyland's studio, there are two floor-to-ceiling bespoke shelves with more ceramics (pp.30–31). They are centre stage, flaunting their different personalities. If they could talk, I imagine they would say 'Hello?' in a raised and surprised tone. 'Why has no one shown us off?'

The first time I saw Hoyland's ceramics was in 2020. At the time, I was exhibiting my largest sculpture to date, *Kingpin* (2020), at the Stand-point Gallery in London. I had been driven by the desire to make an amor-phous sculpture that appeared to be mutating but held conviction. Here Hoyland, a painter, managed to achieve all that I had been striving to do. His ceramics are variform, odd, immediate and funny. I laughed at need-ing every millimetre of my studio to realise *Kingpin* while Hoyland's sculp-tures confidently sat at a manageable scale. I remarked how contemporary the work looked, as if it had just been made.

A selection of these ceramics was exhibited in 1994, at the CCA Galleries in London, the same year they were made. Hoyland wrote an intro-duction to the show (see fig.1, p.15) describing the work as 'these mad little hybrids'. As well as giving it its title, Hoyland's statement also informed the curation of the current exhibition by categorising its themes – idea versus outcome; colour; irony and humour; hybridity – and relating them to the work of other sculptors. The sculptors in the show are: Caroline Achaintre, Eric Bainbridge, Phyllida Barlow, Olivia Bax, Hew Locke, Anna Reading, Jessi Reaves, Andrew Sabin, John Summers and Chiffon Thomas.

Sculpture is harder than it looks: idea versus outcome
Despite the Hoyland sculptures appearing effortless, it is oddly reassuring that he found making them difficult. Between 1976 and 1978, Andrew Sabin trained and traded as a potter in London and Europe before turning to sculpture. After seeing Hoyland's ceramics in 2022, Sabin recreated a few of them in his own studio in an attempt to discover the opportunities that the works provoked:

> *first came the stacking exercises, three or four solid shapes pressed one on top of the other, their weight coming down on a pyramidical base. Then there are a group of works that lift the main body off the ground, still employing a base, but giving lightness and air to how the work finds itself in space. From this follows a series of ever more com-plex lines in space, loops of clay lending support to other loops, some even abandoning the base and using ceramic lines to create stability. Alongside these are a series of ever more complex slab works where the build-up is of flat shapes pressed together, sometimes parallel some-times at angles, to form jagged outlines.*[1]

The sculptors in this exhibition share a desire to answer questions that are difficult to articulate in any other way save by making sculpture. The finished work may clarify some concerns that drove the initial mak-ing but inevitably triggers further questions, therefore the cycle continues. Phyllida Barlow insisted that her work did not have a subject; it was dis-covered through making. What was 'hard' about the medium for Barlow was its absurdity: 'it occupies space, which in a crowded world would be better occupied by things that could serve people either more discreetly or in a better way. Sculpture stands vulnerable to attack for its absolutely unequivocal uselessness, and that to me is its tremendous strength'.[2]

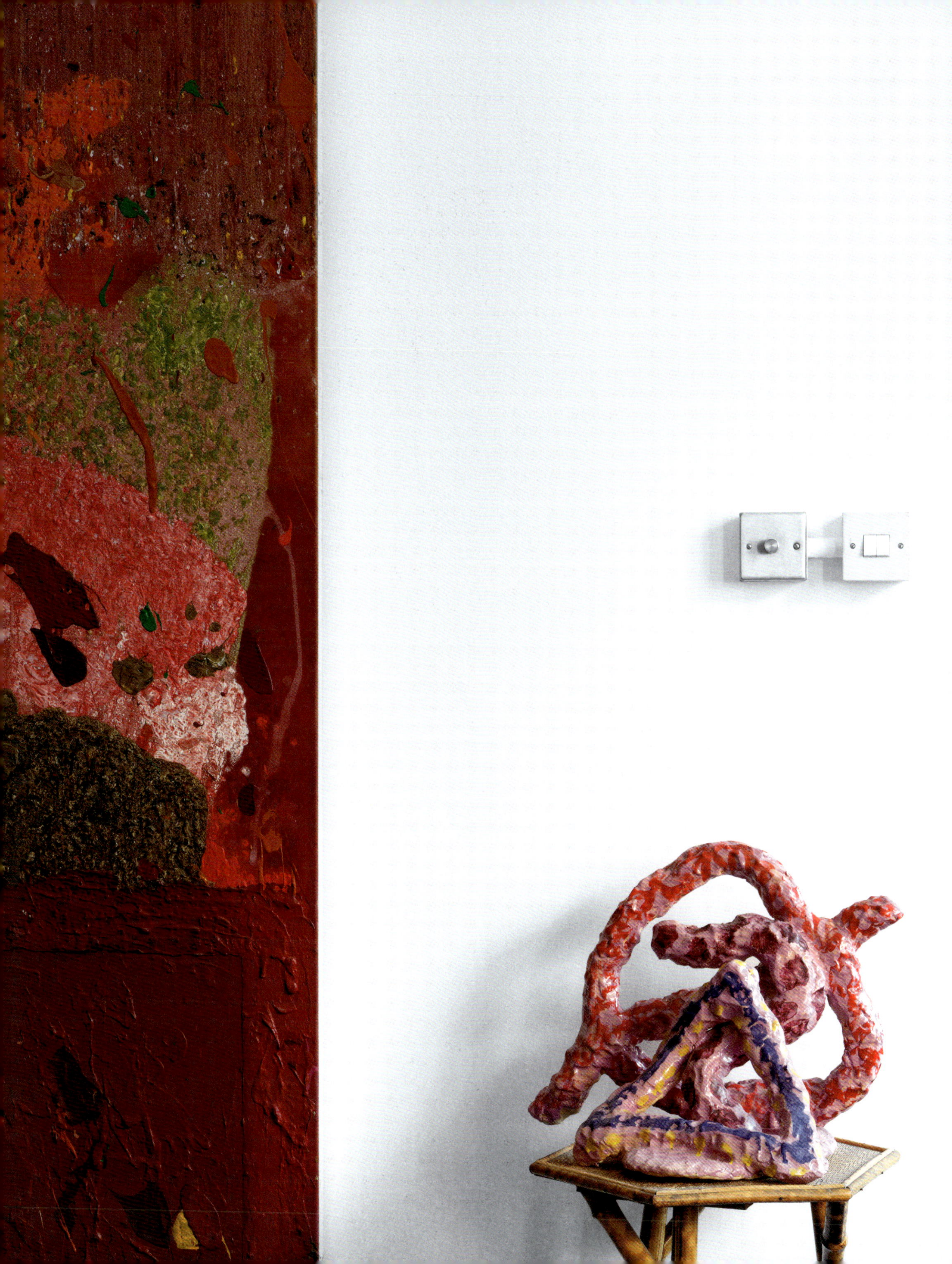

Like Hoyland, Barlow found clay liberating. She claimed that discovering it changed her life. She remembered her early tutors at the Chelsea School of Art (1960–63), Elisabeth Frink and George Fullard, quoting French sculptor Germaine Richier: 'Clay is a hysterical medium. The more you touch it, the more it screams'.[3] Caroline Achaintre endorses working quickly with clay in order to make the piece look malleable, soft and more alive.[4] Sabin decided that Hoyland's

> *rapidly produced ceramic sculptures seem to me to be a speedy run through the basic principles of how objects meet the ground, find their place in space and thereby express differences in character. Their scale is satisfyingly large and the surface shows a quick, unfussy, vigour in the task of getting an idea done and moving on to the next one.*[5]

Barlow's *untitled: badplace; 2020 lockdown 4* (2020, pp.77–81) was part of a collection of sculptures made in her home studio during the Covid-19 pandemic. It employs forms we associate with Barlow's work – a ladder, a flag, stairs, sticks, boulders – which are, of course, all 'Barlowised'. After a string of wildly ambitious installations including at Tate Britain (2014) and the Venice Biennale (2017), Barlow wanted to refresh her approach and return to making singular objects that could unfold and develop in the studio, so revealing themselves as they were being made. Despite its title, in *badplace* positivity is at play. It was made in private, without needing to plan or pre-explain. The sculpture seems too big for the steel support. The makeshift, ad hoc top dominates the sensible, fabricated bottom. The useless sculpture has triumphed.

Unexpected results with colour: colour is material

Hoyland's fixation with colour spilt over from painting to sculpture. I suspect that he enjoyed the apparent capriciousness of colourless glazes. Their magic happens out of sight, baking in the kiln. When the kiln door opened for the second or third time, the wild hotchpotch of contrasting tones would have been revealed. We can see some coloured glazes repeated across sculptures but the layering is unique in each work. 'Hoyland's favoured tool for animation is the dot, the spot and the blotch of colour with which perhaps two thirds of the surfaces are densely populated'.[6]

Historically, colour has been contentious in sculpture. Despite an understanding that Greek sculptures were in fact painted, they are still commonly represented as pure white. Painting a sculpture has been maligned for disguising the true properties of the original material. This is part of the reason why Hoyland's contemporary, Anthony Caro, stopped painting his sculptures bright colours in the 1970s. Presenting the steel naked changed the perception of the work enormously: from light to heavy. Barlow smeared paint, not to unify or disguise a surface but as a structural adhesive. In my studio, discarded household paint helps the consistency of the paper pulp so I can use the material like pre-coloured clay.

In John Summers's sculptures the colour is brash, audacious and cheeky. Summers paints sections gold and throws glitter onto his sculptures. This gives the work a dynamic confidence. Summers commented that Hoyland's glazes looked like 'energetic sketches, unable to sit on the clay but instead they hover, giving the piece a dual identity'.[7] Hoyland used glazes to create movement; Summers uses glitter. Anna Reading described the need to start adding colour to her work when she realised the 'greyness' of cement. She pigments Jesmonite,[8] mixing a colour at a time, then smoothes the coloured material onto the surface with a butter knife. Colour drives the growth of Reading's sculptures; it demands constant reactions and a series of applications over time. For a time in the late 1990s Hew Locke worked with plain cardboard, frustrated with assumptions, based on his British Guyanese background, that he must be concerned with carnival or festivals. Subsequently, he decided to reintroduce colour and embrace the carnivalesque: 'The important thing is that it must look exciting. It must look colourful. It mustn't be boring'.[9]

Andrew Sabin admits that his love affair with colour means he would like it to be as bright as possible. Like Reading's and my own treatment of colour, the pigment is added to liquid material, so the colour *is* the material rather than on it. Colour is not an addition, embellishment or supplement.[10] Sabin pours these materials into three-dimensional obstacle courses (moulds) that are made from containers of various viscosities of margarine. He often uses more than one coloured material at a time so that the flow and interruption is registered on the surface: 'My colours modulate themselves by the experience they have undergone in taking their place like a bruise coming from within'.[11]

Irony and even humour

When I was at art school, I was confronted by a fellow student for not staying the duration of their performance. Indignant, I responded that I do not demand a certain amount of time to look at my sculpture. Sculpture requires engagement from different perspectives, and insisting on attention from multiple directions is greedy. I decided that it was essential to have empathy as a sculptor and sculpture-viewer. Many nineteenth-century philosophers had already trodden this ground: Robert Vischer invented the word *Einfühlung* ('feeling into') in 1873 to describe projecting oneself onto another body, environment or object. Empathy in relation to aesthetics was subsequently discussed by others, including Theodor Lipps, Vernon Lee, Sigmund Freud and Martin Heidegger. Empathy with inanimate objects has birthed the more recent *Object-Oriented Ontology* (OOO) by Graham Harman, which is a current art-school classic.[12] Debate and criticism of art are facilitated when objects are considered autonomous. Even though there are often contradictory viewpoints, it is worthwhile contemplating sculpture from the inside (material) to the outside (form).

Sabin scoops margarine out of large vats, *feeling into* the negative space. We cannot see the back of Achaintre's tufted wall-works, which are also made from the reverse, shooting wool yarn through a vertically stretched canvas. I watched a video of Barlow in her studio sticking her hand inside a plaster sculpture. She looks unsatisfied then, after a sigh, pushes the work off the bench and it crashes to the floor along with all preciousness.[13] The puncturing of pretence was funny. The day before I was due to visit Summers's studio, he called to warn me that his space looked like 'a forest of shit'. This was funny. Sabin's account of ordering hundreds of boxes of margarine from a factory in Scotland was funny. If an artist can laugh at the ridiculousness of their activity, it helps to establish the genuineness of their work.

Barlow believed that the more a sculpture is named (reducing it to an image description), the more it makes the work's physicality and materiality redundant.[14] Harman uses the joke to explain his OOO philosophy in relation to art: a joke (like an artwork) cannot be paraphrased or explained because by doing so it is ruined. When a joke is made, pleasure is produced by the disjunction between duration and the instant, where we experience the slow passing of time and a sudden, fleeting climax. A joke stretches time like an elastic band. We know the elastic will snap, we just do not know when, and we find that anticipation rather pleasurable.[15] Jokes rely on a certain amount of indirect knowledge. Artists are familiar with indirect knowledge; they gain it through making. All the sculptures in this exhibition simultaneously show endurance and presence; they hold us in suspense.

Sculptures are as diverse as jokes: they can be hilarious, self-assured and sharp, or disturbing, vulnerable and blundering. During a conversation with Reading, she spoke of her embarrassment of using oyster shells: 'they make me cringe'. Reading has used shells before as a material to clad sculptures. In *Bouquet* (2022, pp.100–3), shells are not on the surface but neatly hung on fishing wire. When I teach at art schools, students often use fishing wire because they expect it to be invisible. This makes *me* cringe – it is not! Reading uses it discerningly, through a long-standing interest in sea creatures and fishing. She has many fishing flies in her studio and some have found their way onto sculptures. She explains that their deceptively beautiful colouration is in fact rather perverse because they are made of dead animals. Reading has painstakingly covered the metal bar in *Bouquet* with embroidery thread. She wants people to see the labour: laughing at her meticulousness might allow the sculpture to be taken more seriously.

Robert Garnett's essay 'Beyond Irony: Humour, Painting and the Funny-Peculiar'[16] sets out the difference between irony and humour. Irony is exclusive, whereas humour is inclusive. Irony is critical and to understand it one has to be in on the joke. Despite how complex Hoyland's ceramics were to make, they have a pleasing, self-assured naivety. It is deceptively hard to pull off the 'right kind of wrongness'.[17] Jessi Reaves's work is a good example. Reaves had a brief stint studying furniture design before switching to painting. When she graduated from Rhode Island School of Design in 2010 she moved to New York, where she got a part-time job as an upholsterer. Her understanding of design and how to make functional objects allows her to play with materials and construction principles in her sculptures. Reaves is interested in figuring out how to do something the wrong way; in feeling emboldened to take on building something without the right tool; in not planning ahead.[18]

Reaves's *Three Bowl Table* (2019, pp.98–99) appears at first glance like a table and chairs set for a meal, but on closer inspection the work is inside-out. The chairs' internal structure is exposed revealing the guts: foam and wood. The wooden bowls are underneath the glass rather than on top. Reaves's sculptures mock our sheep-like obsession with design trends. Isamu Noguchi's iconic modernist coffee table, created for Herman Miller in 1947 and described in the original catalogue as 'sculpture-for-use' and 'design for production', has been a particularly significant point of reference for Reaves.[19] Her sculptures sit like (un)practical jokes. They laugh at themselves too because, after all, they are artworks: arguably the most precious and snobbish of all objects.

Humour can also be unsettling. Achaintre considers the wool material in her work to have an intense and uncanny eeriness.[20] Chiffon Thomas gravitates towards objects that have had a life of their own, manipulating and playing with their contexts. Thomas likes 'spinning stuff on its head… tweak[ing] something and that's usually enough to bring uncanniness through'.[21] Summers's sculptures demand a smile because there is something troubling and unknown about what we are seeing. In *Mud and Stars, Gold Head* (2022, pp.95–96), there is a comically large sock on an equally large leg and foot. The leg and one hand are frighteningly lifelike under smudges and stains of other material. The figure's head is stuck, reclined and looking upwards as if it has been frozen by the weight of the ridiculous sock.

Hew Locke is celebrated for using humour and satire to position himself politically as a cultural insider rather than an excluded outsider.[22] Locke's work is festooned with icons of British hierarchy, ironically dissecting the pomp but also brutally reminding us of man's historic and relentless corruption of power. Eric Bainbridge's work teases sculptural hierarchies, subverting the monumentality of artists such as Henry Moore and Anthony Caro. Irony endures if the criticism remains relevant for different generations. If irony is considered surface level, then irony with humour combined can penetrate. A consideration of a surface or skin is what preoccupied Bainbridge in the 1980s–90s, when he covered timber and steel armatures in fur. He is curious about throwaway consumerist objects, so blows up their forms and then obscures them with synthetic fabric (pp.72–74). Bainbridge reflected in an interview with Penelope Curtis: 'I don't know whether it is a particular British thing that if you make something that employs humour, it can't be serious. I've never felt like that…I've always seen humour as another strategy to deal with the world, with life'.[23]

These (mad) little hybrids

Sculpture borrows from and overlaps with other disciplines. Reaves's work teeters between furniture and sculpture and by doing so she challenges both fine art and design boundaries. Thomas spent two years learning stop–motion animation while he was an undergraduate student at the Art Institute of Chicago (graduated 2014). This informed an interest in analogue making and taking on multiple roles – characters, set, lighting and production – which have inevitably influenced narrative-building in his work. Achaintre trained as a blacksmith before studying art. Her current techniques – tapestry, ceramic and watercolour – have long and complex histories that interweave with craft practices. Achaintre is more interested in their material properties than their histories. She describes her tufted wall-work as a 'kind of a three-dimensional woollen painting'.[24]

In 2008, the exhibition *Against Nature: The Hybrid Forms of Modern Sculpture* at the Henry Moore Institute showed how sculptors' interest in metamorphic and fantastical forms led to various mutations of the figure. This collision of the human with animal, vegetable or machine was most prominent in the late 1940s and early 1950s when sculptors were keen to articulate new statements about post-war society.[25] Today, we might recognise a minotaur or hippogriff, and we understand hybrid cars. The easy assimilation of such hybrids is due to our familiarity with the separate components, and our comprehending of them as a combined, single entity. *These Mad Hybrids* demonstrates how broad and complex the components in sculpture-making have become. The sculptors do not rely on homogenising forms by using just one material (bronze), but instead embrace differences and contradictions.

Summers identified two camps in Hoyland's ceramics. The first he described as being concise and recognisable, like a figure or a kettle. The second he thought were harder to name and looked more spontaneous.[26] In Summers's *High Ground* (2023, pp.94, 97), a feminine-looking face is partially obscured by an elaborate gold mask. The bust is held up by scaffold poles, replacing arms with a more sturdy and solid structure. She is part human, part architectural prop. In Thomas's *Grounded* (2021, pp.104–5), a face is suspended with metal rebar wire, normally used to keep steel bars in position while concrete is poured. Coloured threads weave in and out, as if the face is unravelling. Thomas calls his work 'impossible bodies', describing both the materials and their new contexts, as well as the artist's desire to create something beyond the purview of nature or belief.[27] In Achaintre's *Cruizer* (2019, pp.69, 71), the removal of two perfect circles creates a face: 'Masks have a life in themselves. I think it's the characters or potential bearers of the masks or what story they are telling that is interesting; what could potentially be behind them'.[28]

Locke's sculpture *The Kingdom of the Blind* (2008, pp.86–89) is a frieze of totemic figures. The largest is a mythical king: a puppet master who is connected to his subjects with gold chains. Locke's influences are broad: from Renaissance tapestries, Indian temple statues, Hindu sculptures and Egyptian tomb paintings to kitsch plastic toys found in Brixton markets. The range of plastic ephemera used to adorn his sculptures is expansive, highlighting the escalated movement of goods around the globe: fake weaponry, model dinosaurs, dolls, plastic flowers and beads. Locke's sculpture is reminiscent of the Burryman, a figure who parades annually around South Queensferry, near Edinburgh (where Locke was born), becoming enshrouded with burrs. The origins of the Burryman are unknown. Locke's king is mythological but resonates with many realities: child soldiers, inner-city gangs, African wars and the Empire. The anthropomorphic in all these works pulls us back into our own reality: do we recognise these hybrids?

In my sculptures, I often incorporate readymade objects to give a hint of knowing in an otherwise invented structure. In *How do you do* (2019, pp.82–84), a single bicycle handle juts into space. The handle influenced the title of the work after I realised it was an articulation of first meetings, which are impossible to predict; every encounter is different. It is a sculpture anticipating a mixed, hybrid feeling. Sabin's forms bear palpable witness to the entanglement of man and his environment.[29] His sculpture *From Time to Time* (2018, pp.90–93) is a complex hybrid: snake meets spider, meets comb, meets octopus, meets exotic plant. There are numerous legs: some sit firmly on the floor while others are slightly raised. This sculpture is on the move.

Reading's forms are a collision of mammals, birds and sea creatures that become her own animal hybrid (p.103). She uses a variety of organic materials and fuses them with industrial processes. Once assembled and constructed, the materials are themselves a hybrid. In recent conversations with Thomas, we discussed the shortfalls of the word 'assemblage'. It is an accumulative word that does not take into account disassembling. As well as casting, embroidering and arranging, Thomas excavates, dismembers and splices; he does as much subtracting as adding. Calling the process 'hybrid' might invite more questions about the formation, rather than assume the actions performed. Classifications are problematic, which is exactly what Thomas's work questions: the axes of identity, gender and race and where these divisions disappear.

Mad

There has been an explosion of interest in clay over the last decade, as evidenced in survey exhibitions and monographs focusing on the material. Hoyland's work has not been included in these celebrations, which perhaps is just as well; the work has sculptural ambitions beyond the material employed. Hoyland transformed 'hysterical' clay into 'mad' sculptures. Both words share varied meanings, from fanatical to furious.

If we consider mad as a form of exaggeration, then it reveals a shared sensibility in this exhibition. Mad is not mediocre; it is emphatic, enthusiastic and wild. Madness is also a position of precariousness where there is a risk of collapse. There are physical instabilities on display in *These Mad Hybrids*, but there are other more complicated instabilities too. William Shakespeare's clowns and fools are able to expose the reality of life in the most expressive manner through complex humour and truth. For King Lear, his madness allows him to see reason and learn from his mistakes. There is an obvious parallel with making art, where a mistake almost always offers new possibilities. The individual sculptures in *These Mad Hybrids* are colourful and singular, but most importantly, they are unpredictable. They possess their own sets of questions, finding reason through their madness.

1   Andrew Sabin, *Painting and Sculpture – The Spot and Hole*, 2022 (unpublished text, commissioned for this project).

2   Sara Harrison (ed.), *Phyllida Barlow: Collected Lectures, Writings and Interviews*, Hauser & Wirth, London, 2021, p.151.

3   *Ibid.*, p.205.

4   Caroline Achaintre, in Emma Dean (ed.), *Making Trouble*, BALTIC Centre for Contemporary Art, Gateshead and FRAC – Fonds Regional d'Art Contemporain Champagne-Ardenne, Reims, 2016, p.166.

5   Sabin, *op. cit.*

6   *Ibid.*

7   John Summers, *Totem Guardians*, 2022 (unpublished text, commissioned for this project).

8   Jesmonite is the manufacturer's name; the material is a combination of gypsum and water-based acrylic resin.

9   Elizabeth Fullerton, 'Bright Colours, Dark Subjects: Hew Locke's Unsettling Pageant', 2022, https://www.nytimes.com/2022/04/01/arts/design/hew-locke-the-procession-tate-britain.html, accessed 22 September 2023.

10 David Batchelor, *Chromophobia: Ancient and Modern, and Few Notable Exceptions*, The Centre for the Study of Sculpture, Henry Moore Institute, Leeds, 1997, p.2.

11 Sabin, *op. cit.*

12 Graham Harman, *Object-Oriented Ontology: A New Theory of Everything*, Pelican, London, 2018. Harman used the term 'object-oriented philosophy' in his 1999 doctoral dissertation.

13 'Phyllida Barlow: Translating the World Around', Hauser & Wirth, 2023, https://www.youtube.com/watch?v=TM3L-ILNhgw, accessed 29 August 2023.

14 Harrison, *op. cit.*, p.365.

15 Simon Critchley, *On Humour*, Routledge, London, 2002, p.7.

16 Andrew Hunt (ed.), *Painting: Funny Peculiar*, Slimvolume, London, 2020.

17 *Ibid.*, p.77.

18 'Jessi Reaves Leaves it Dirty', interview with Octavia Bürgel, 2021, https://032c.com/magazine/jessi-reaves-leaves-it-dirty, accessed 29 August 2023.

19 Jessica Freeman-Attwood, *android stroll*, exhibition text, Herald Street Gallery, London, 2017, http://www.heraldst.com/jessi-reaves-2017, accessed 23 August 2023.

20 Achaintre, *op. cit.*, p.164.

21 'Chiffon Thomas by Troy Montes Michie', *Bomb* Magazine, 2023, https://bombmagazine.org/articles/chiffon-thomas-by-troy-montes-michie/, accessed 25 August 2023.

22 Melissa Chemam, 'Hew Locke's "The Procession": Transforming Darkness into Joy', *Art UK*, 2022, https://artuk.org/discover/stories/hew-lockes-the-procession-transforming-darkness-into-joy, accessed 30 September 2023.

23 Eric Bainbridge, *Steel Sculptures*, Camden Arts Centre, London, 2012. p.52.

24 Achaintre, *op. cit.*, p.164.

25 Penelope Curtis and Stephen Feeke (eds.), *Against Nature: The Hybrid Forms of Modern Sculpture*, Henry Moore Institute, Leeds, 2008. p.53. Most of the sculptures in the exhibition were black or brown bronze, which shows how hybridity in sculpture has expanded since then.

26 Summers, *op. cit.*

27 'Chiffon Thomas by Troy Montes Michie', *op. cit.*

28 Achaintre, *op. cit.*, p.164.

29 Andrew Sabin, *An Installation of New Works*, Chisenhale Gallery, London, 1990, p.2.

Exhibition

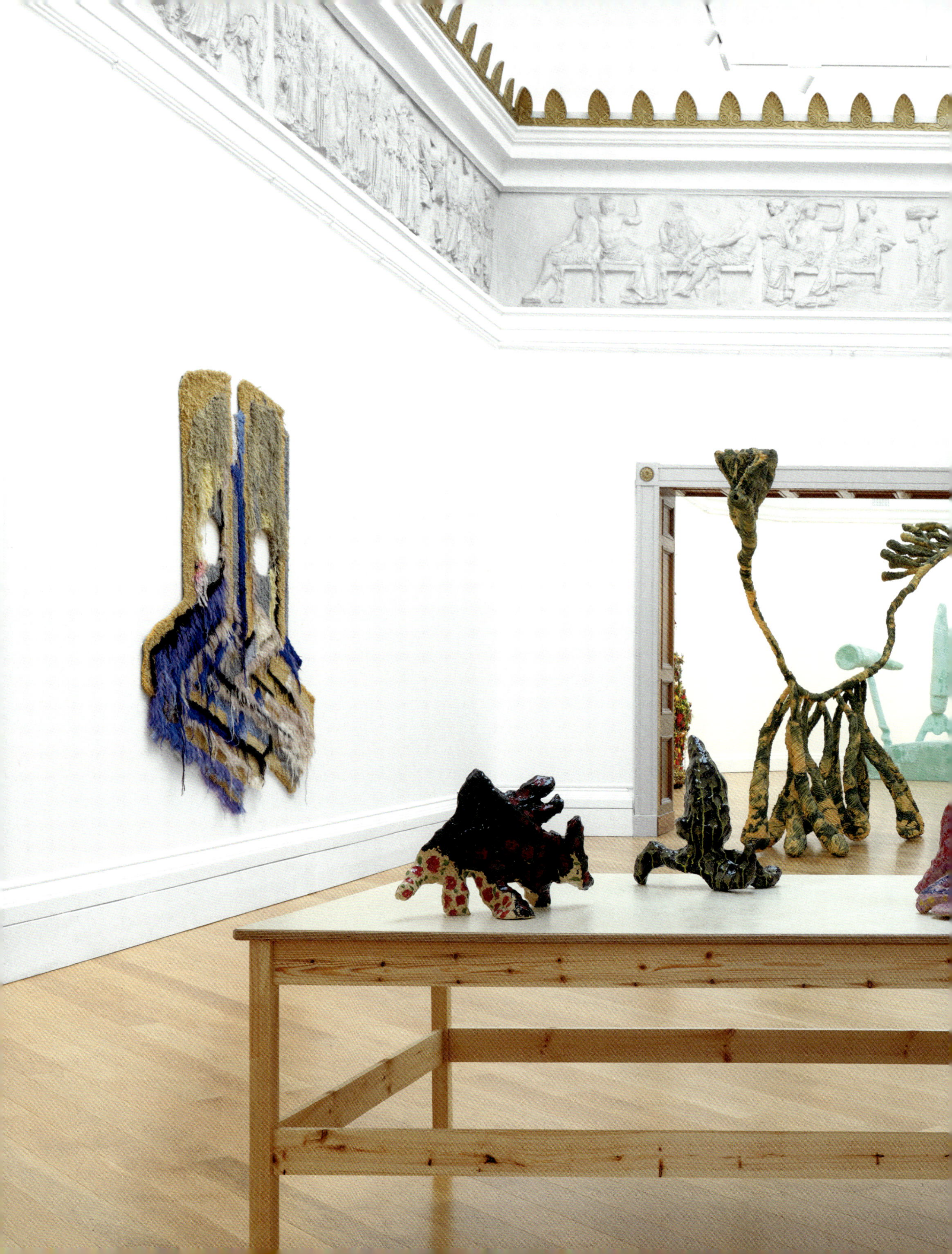

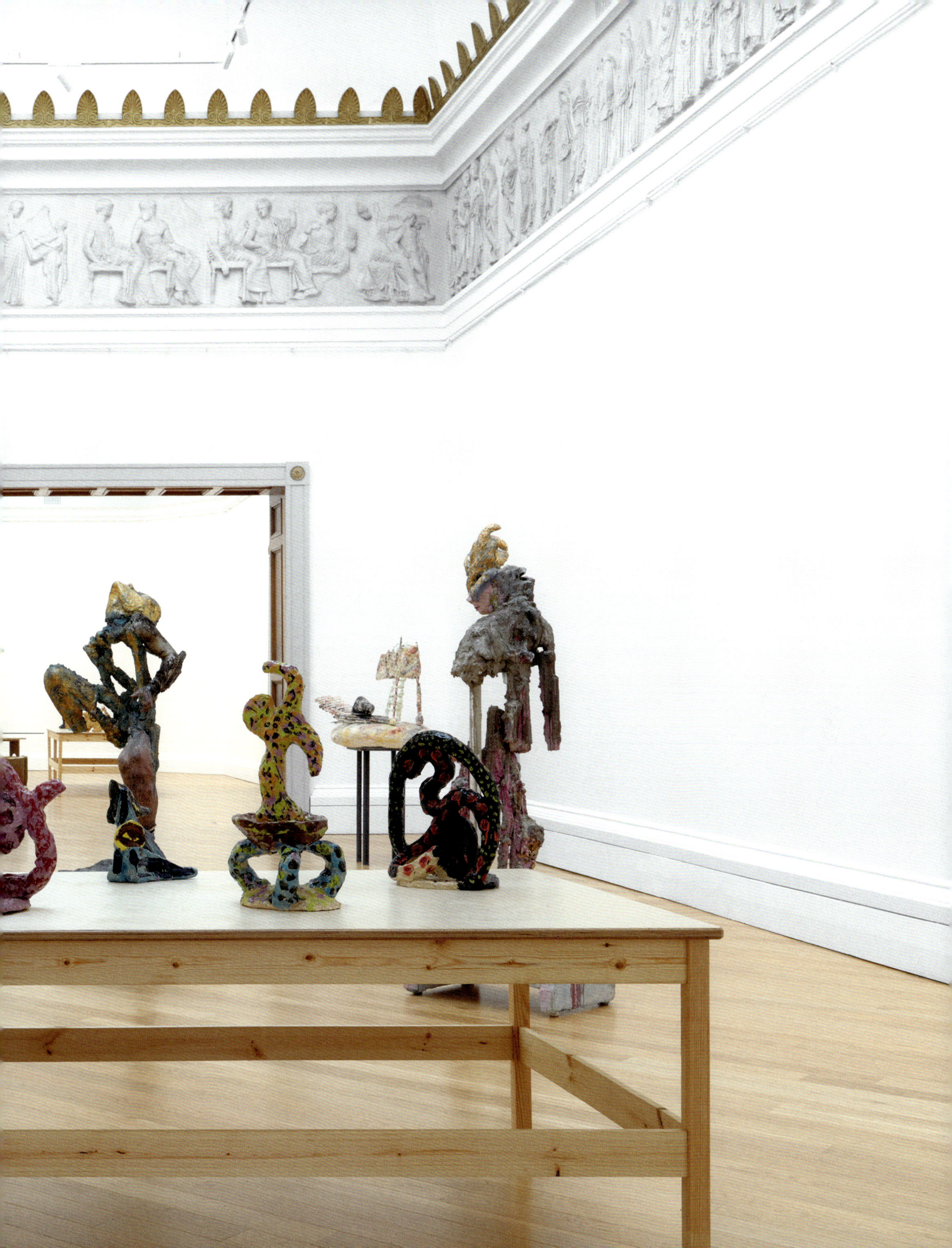

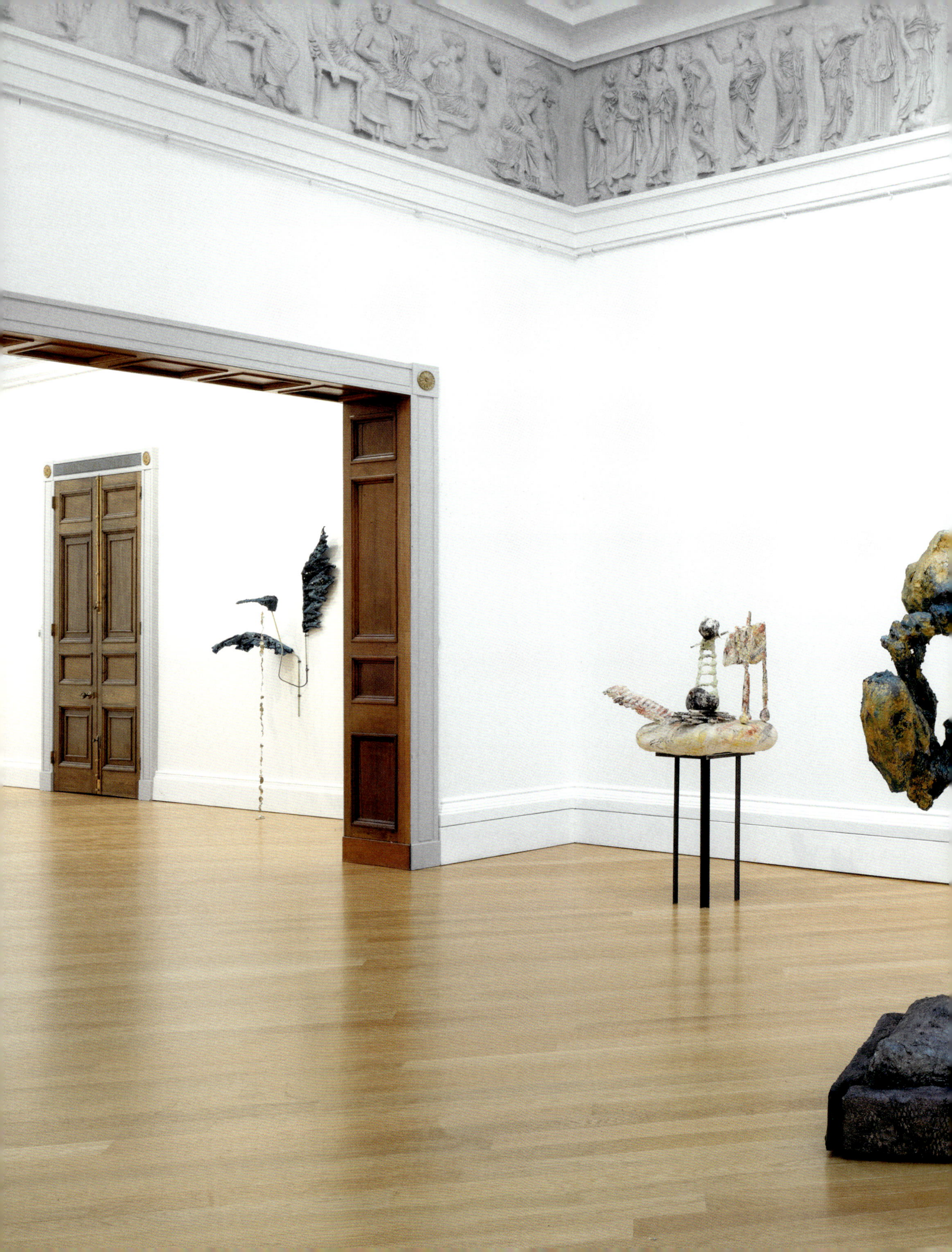

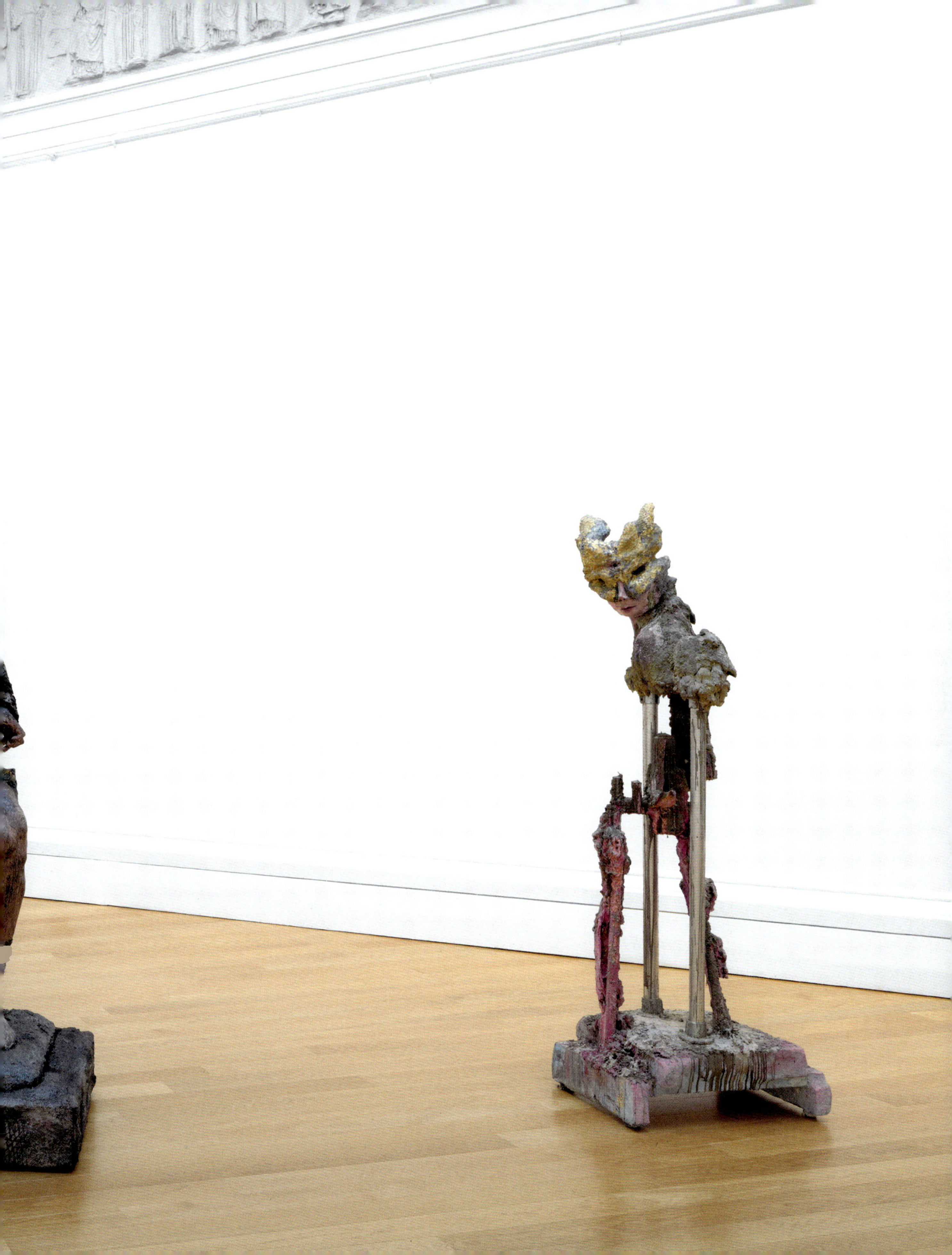

Caroline Achaintre, *Cruizer*, 2019
Tufted wool, 256 × 220 cm

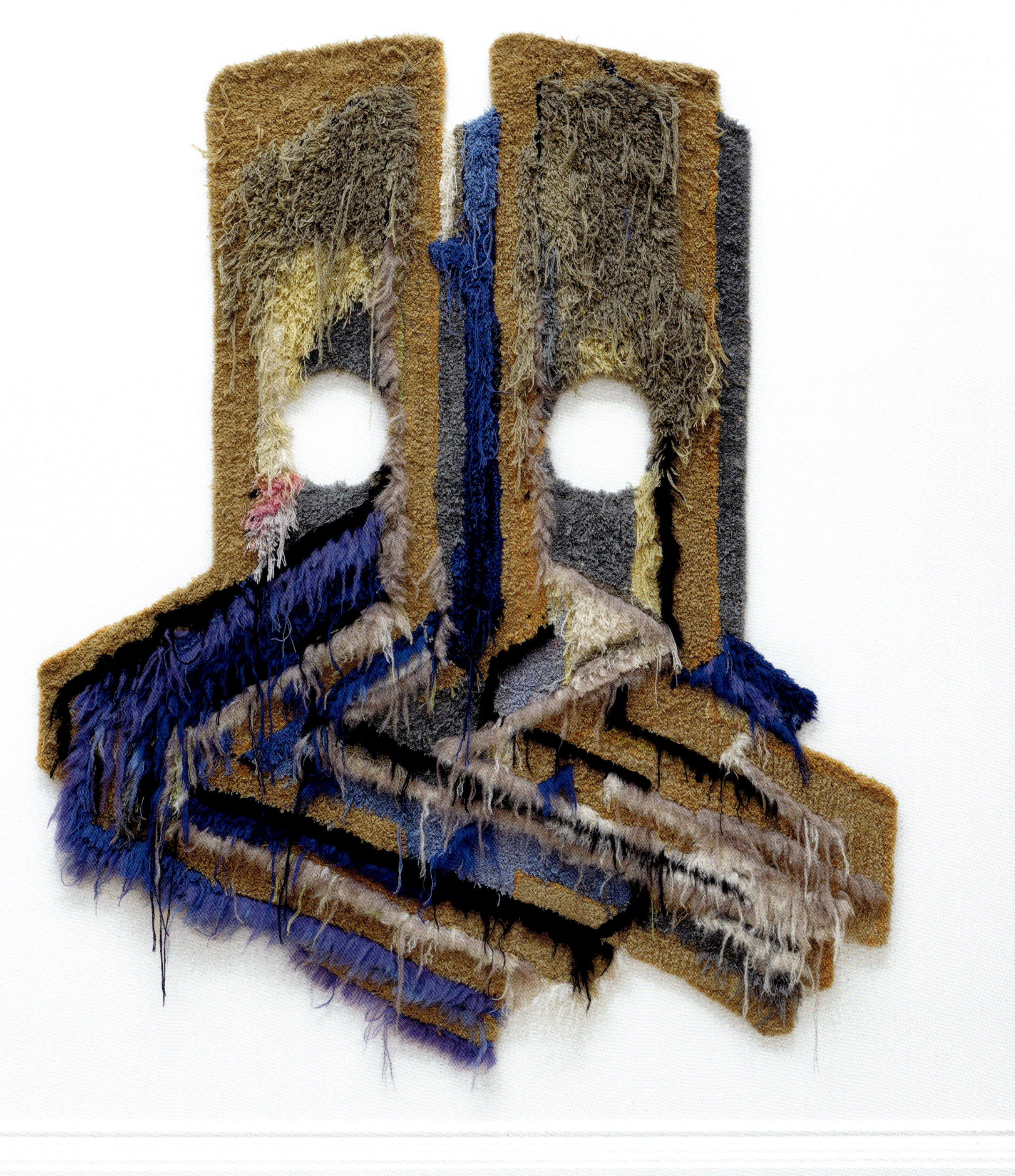

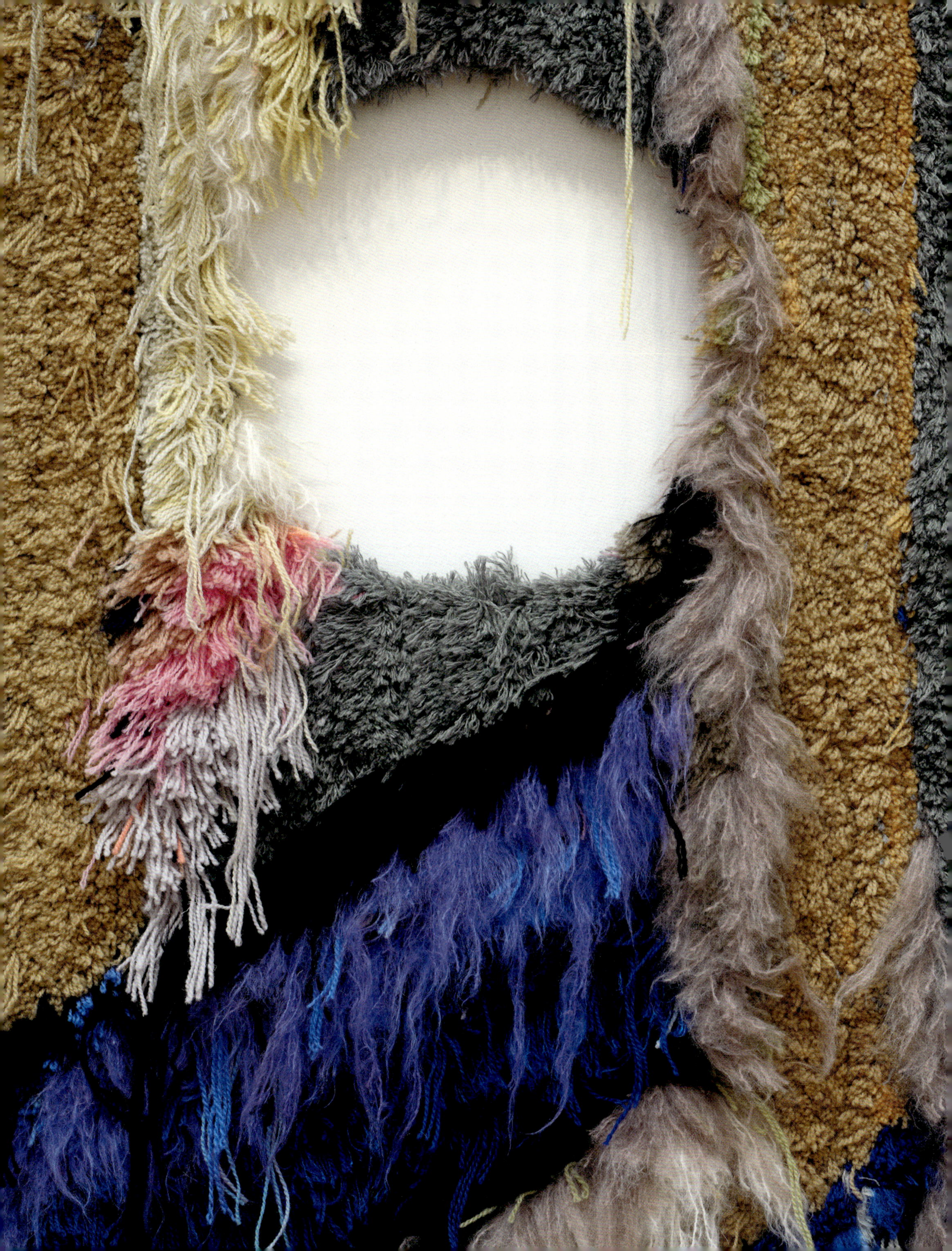

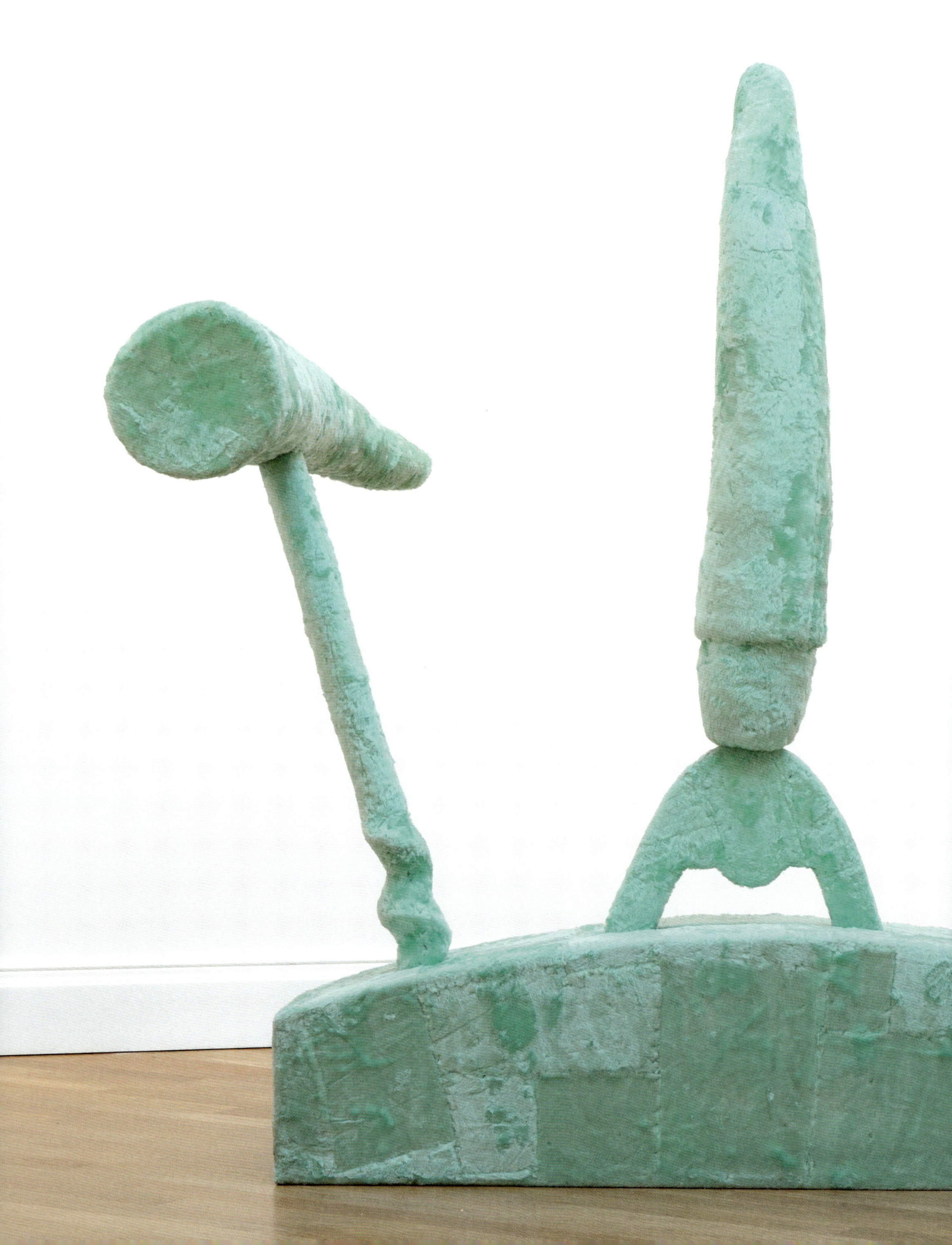

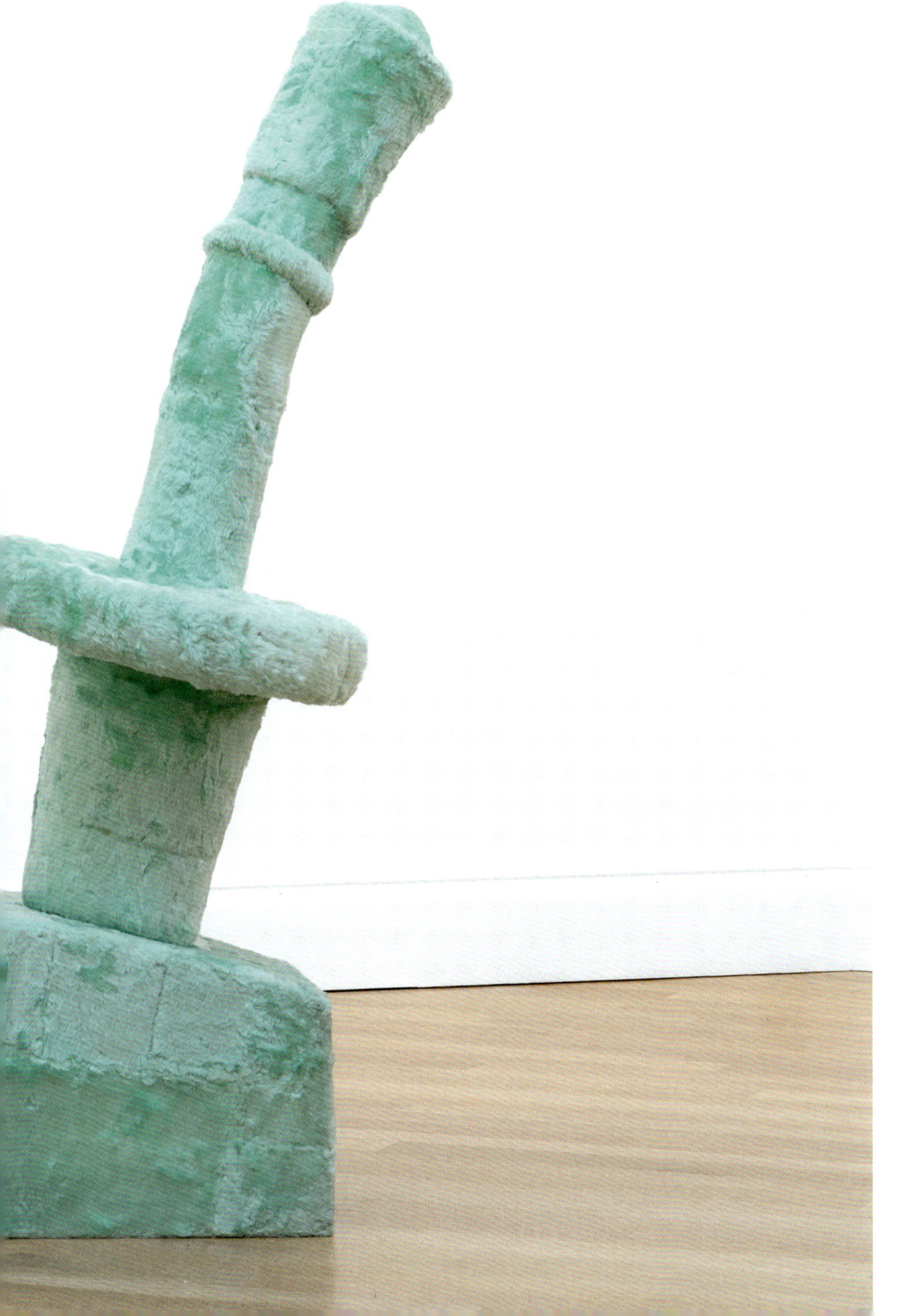

Eric Bainbridge, *Made in Hong Kong*, 1987
Fur fabric, plaster, timber, steel
and wire mesh, 276.9 × 320 × 170.2 cm

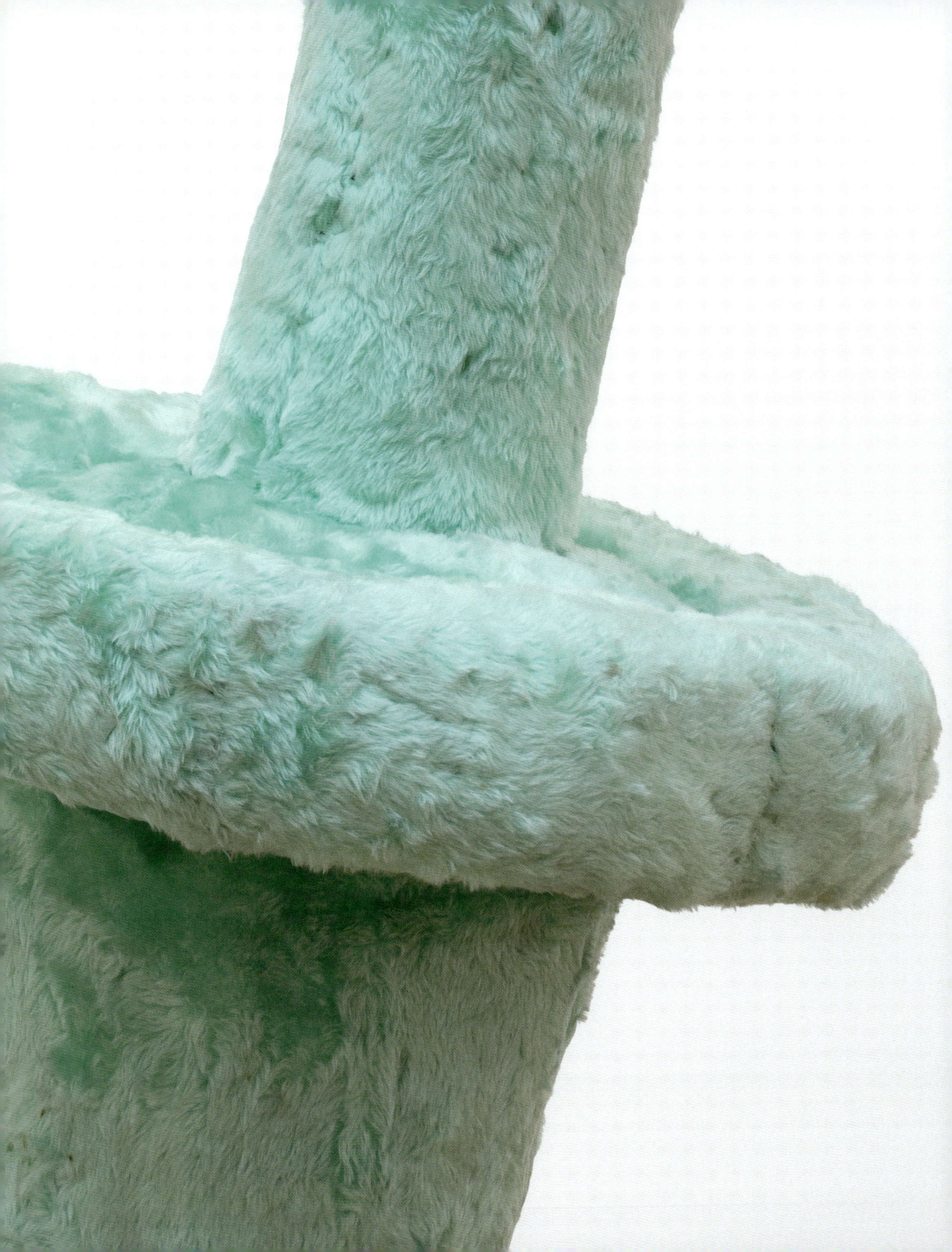

Phyllida Barlow, *untitled: badplace;*
2020 lockdown 4, 2020
Plywood, wire netting, polyurethane
foam, scrim, PVA, plaster cement,
paint and steel, 172.3 × 82 × 75.5 cm

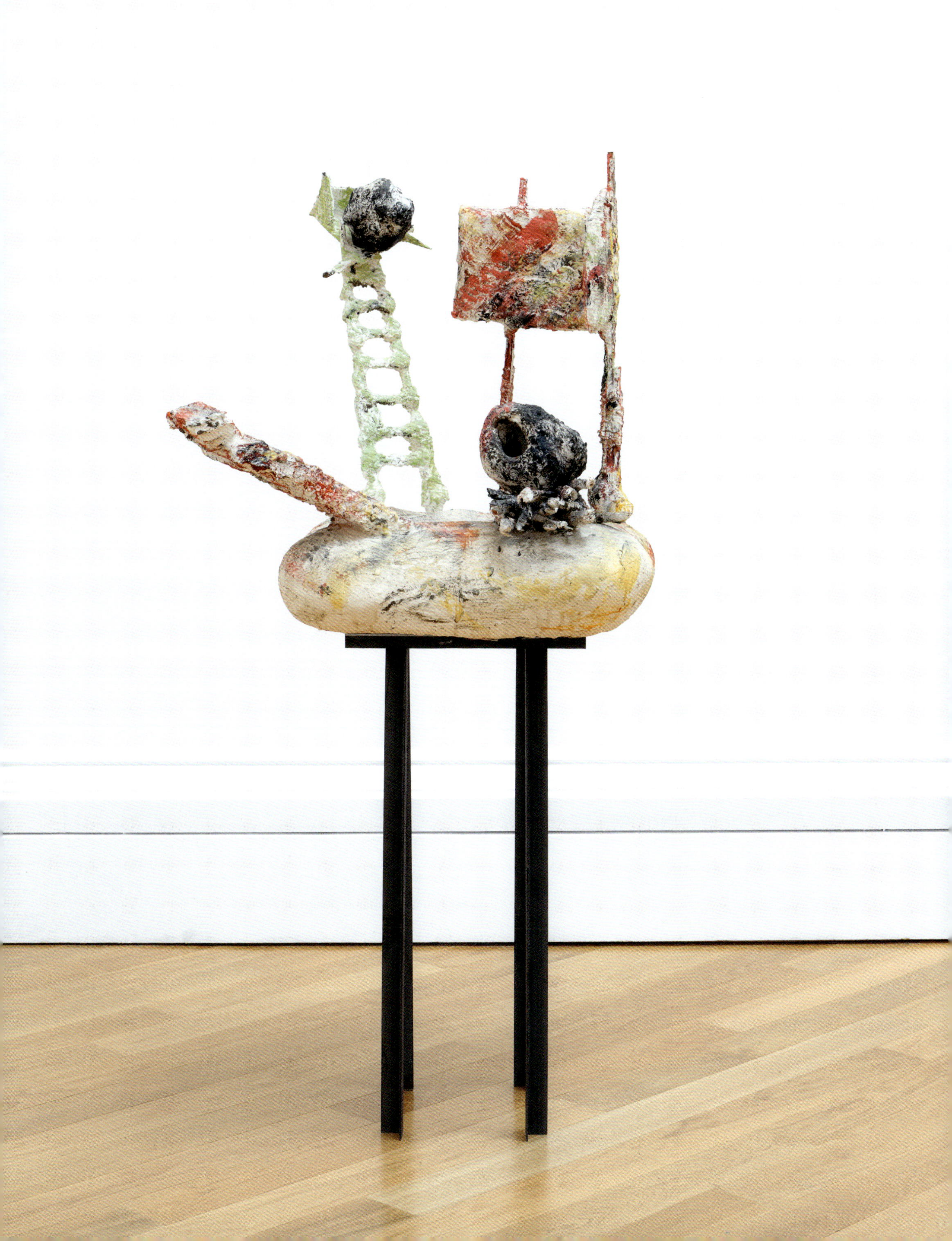

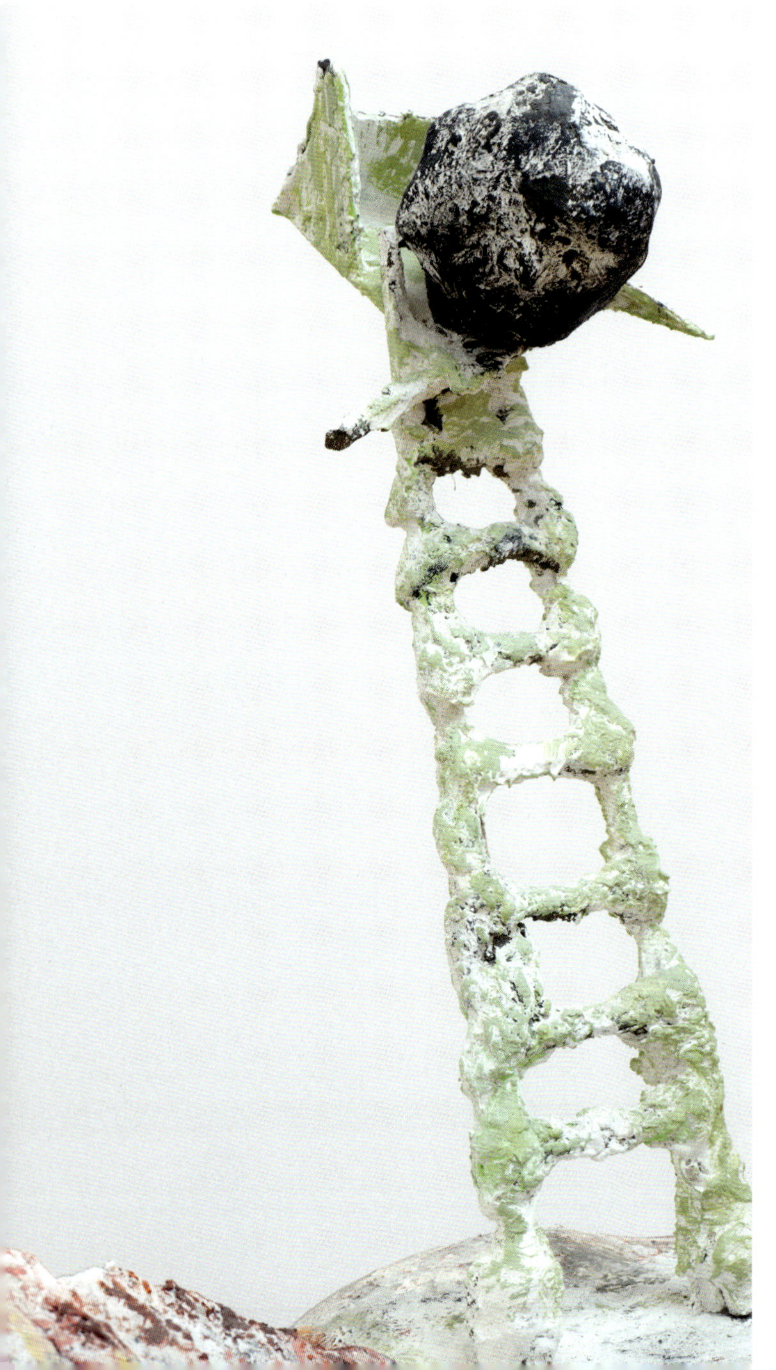

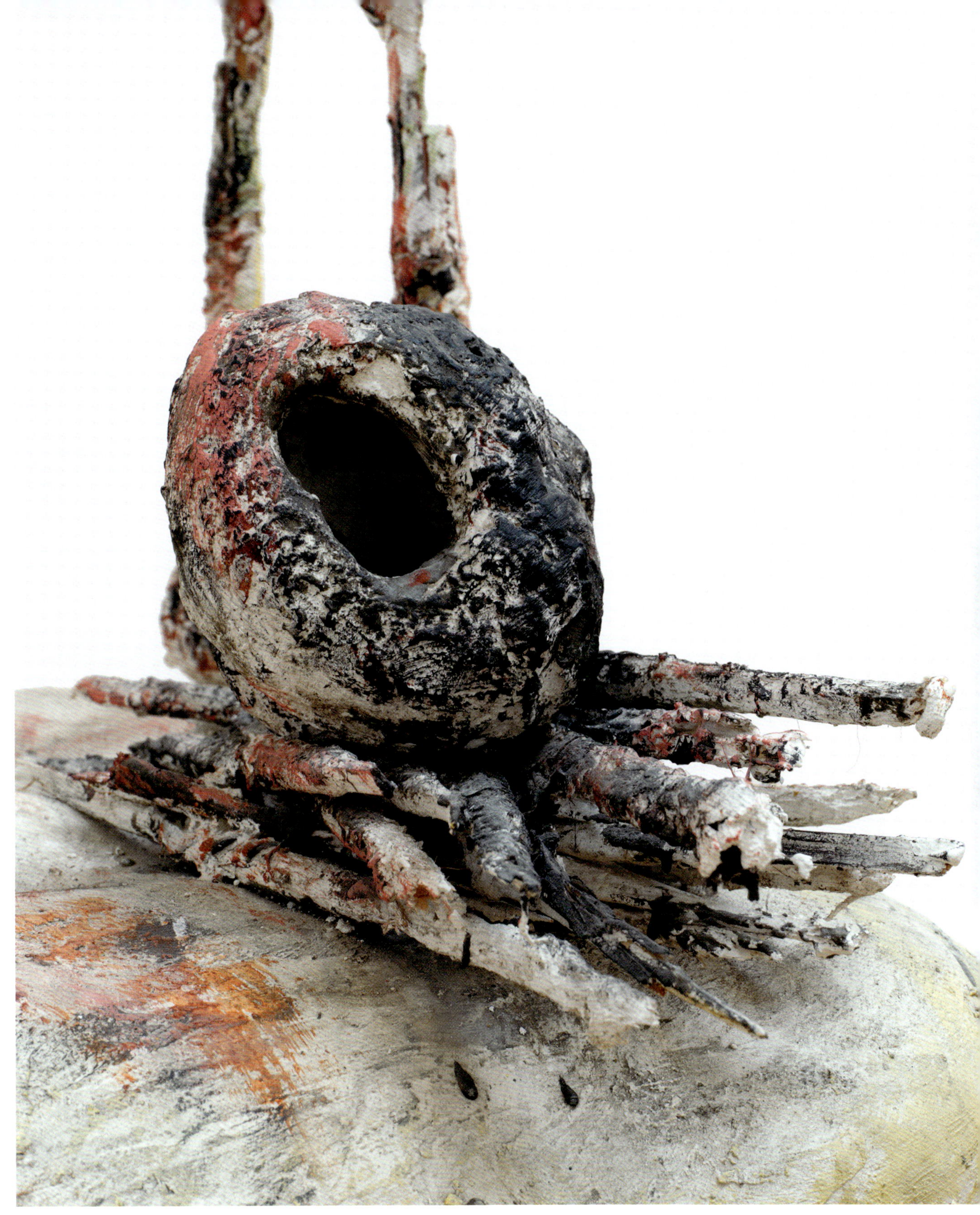

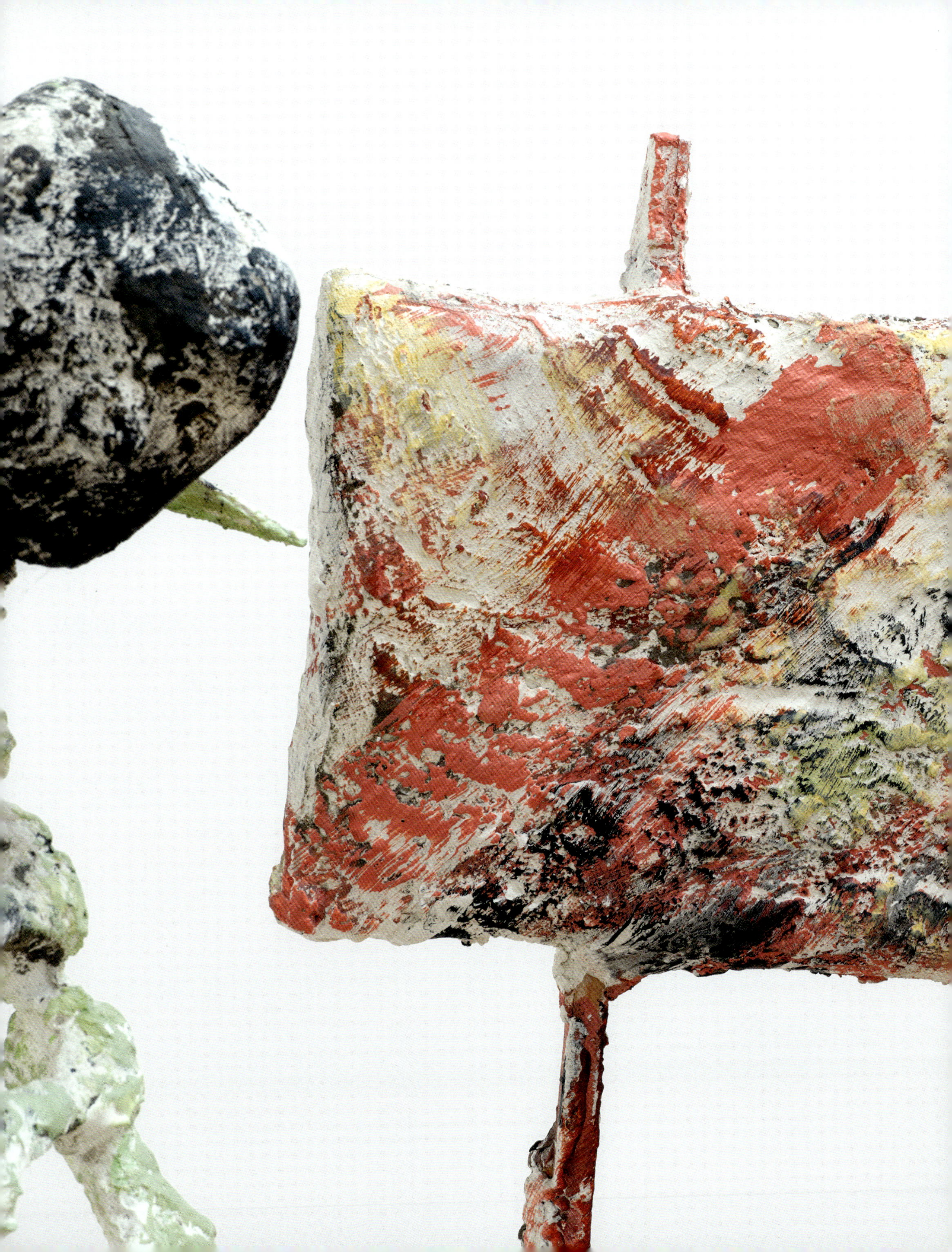

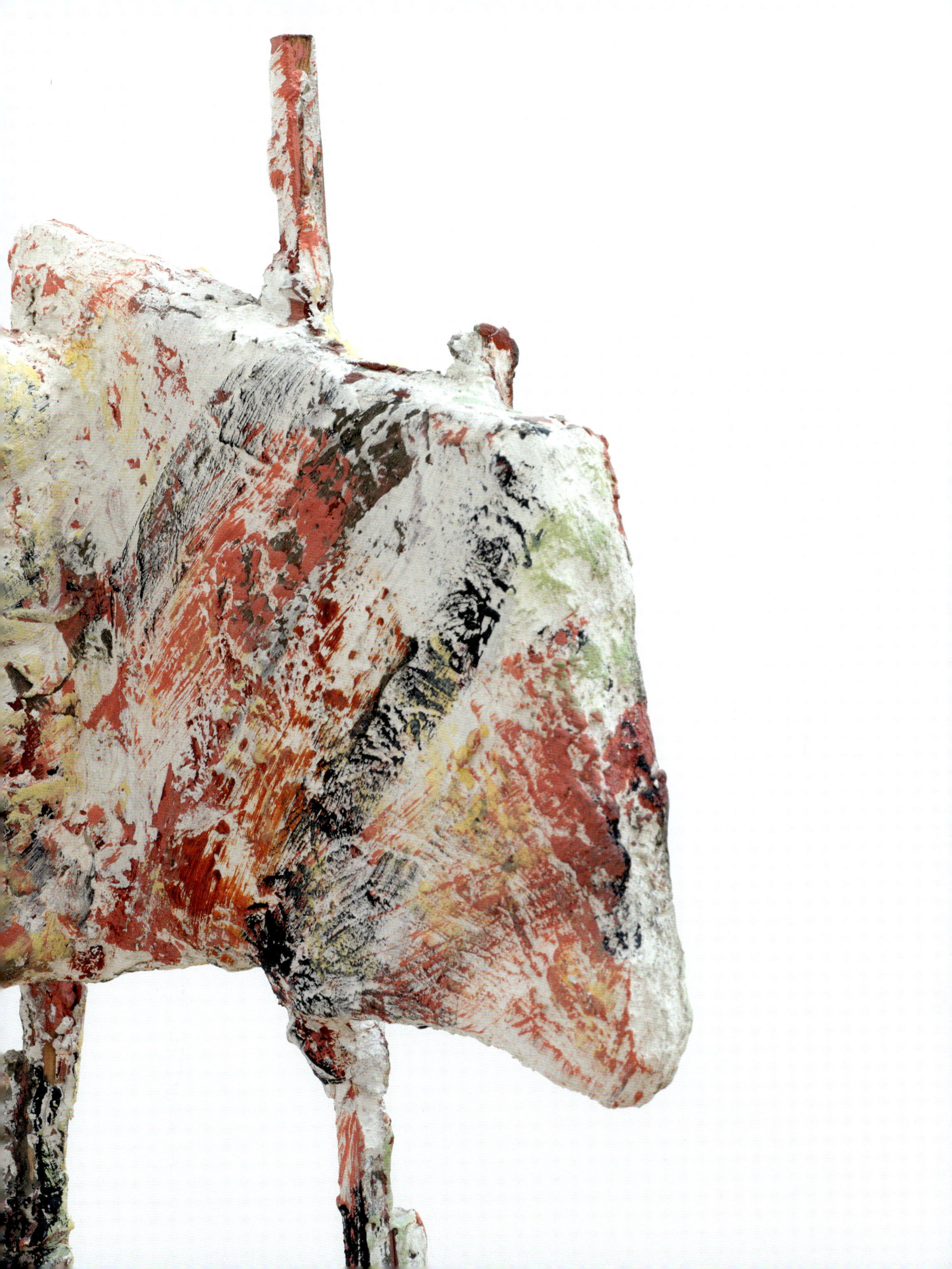

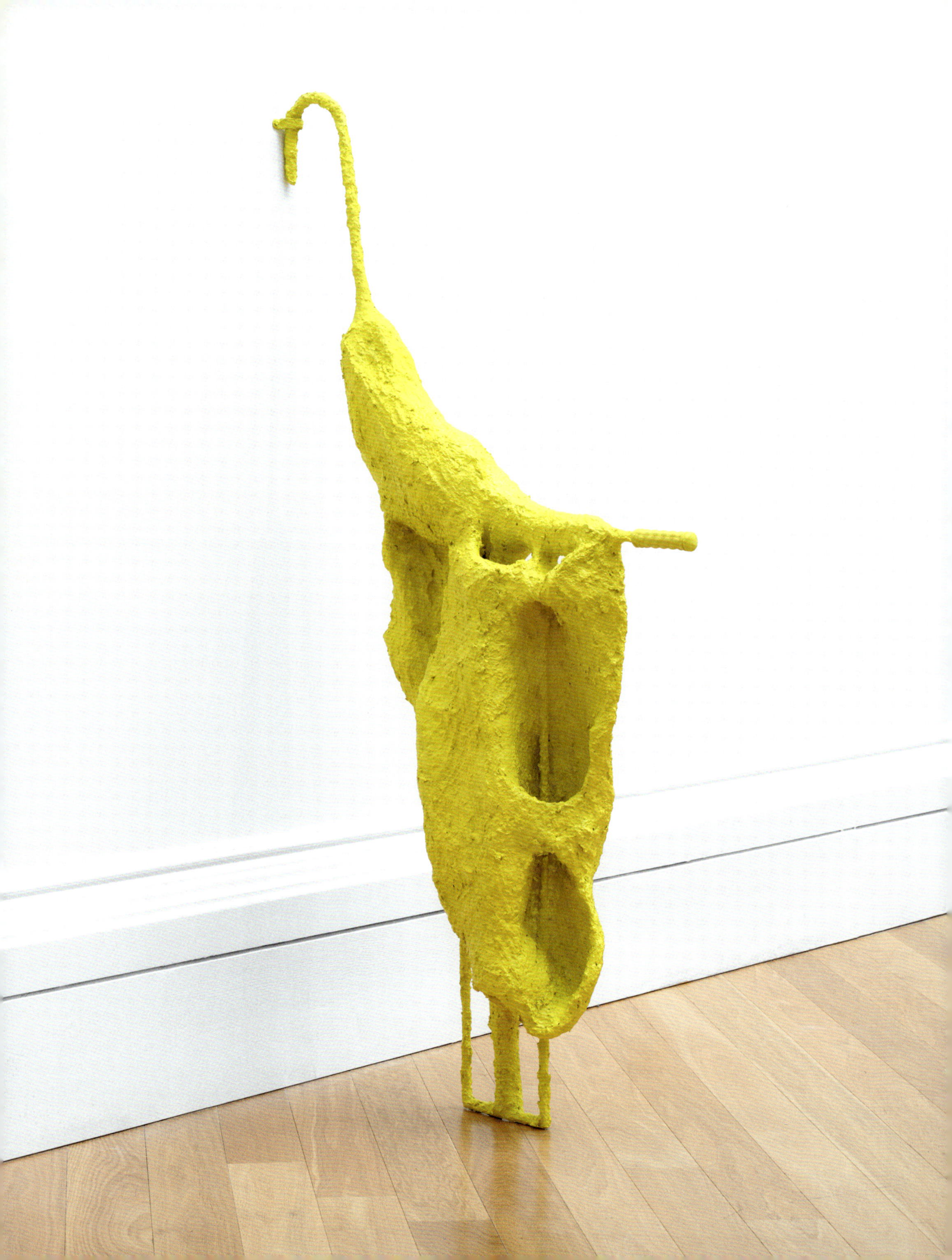

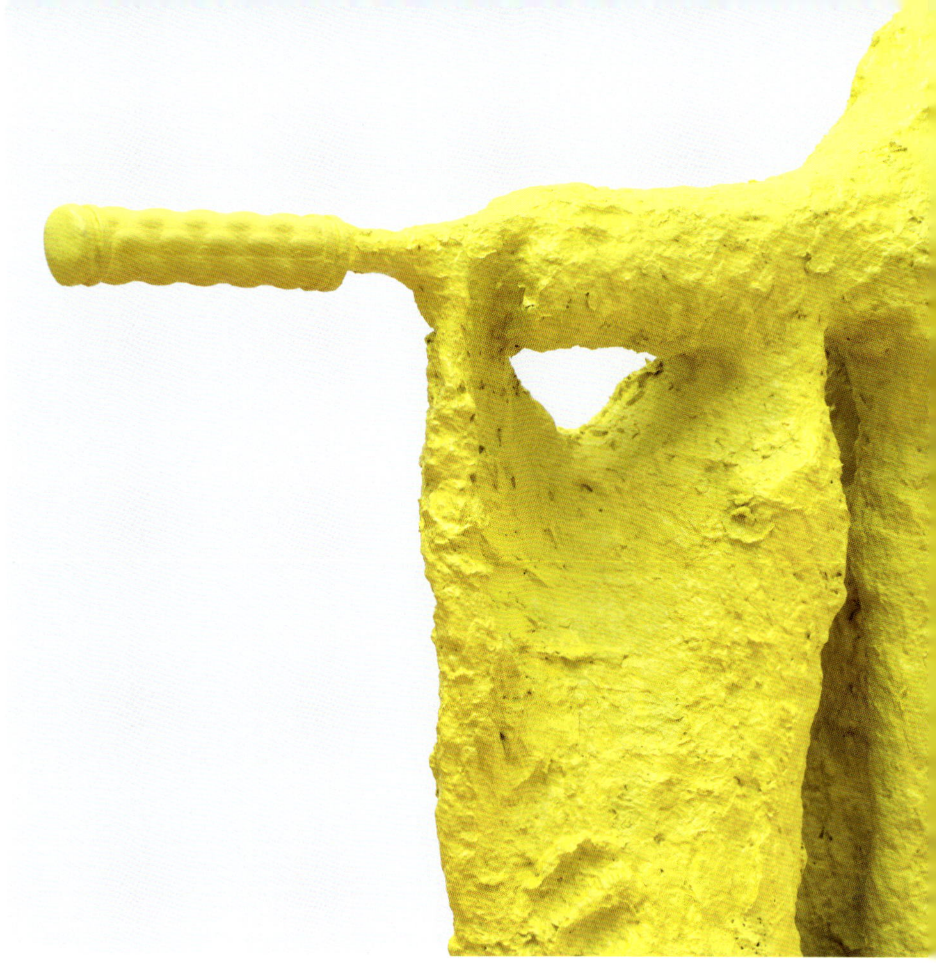

Olivia Bax, *How do you do*, 2019
Steel, chicken wire, newspaper,
UV resistant PVA, household paint,
plaster, UV varnish, fixing, handle
and milliput, 174 × 96 × 20 cm

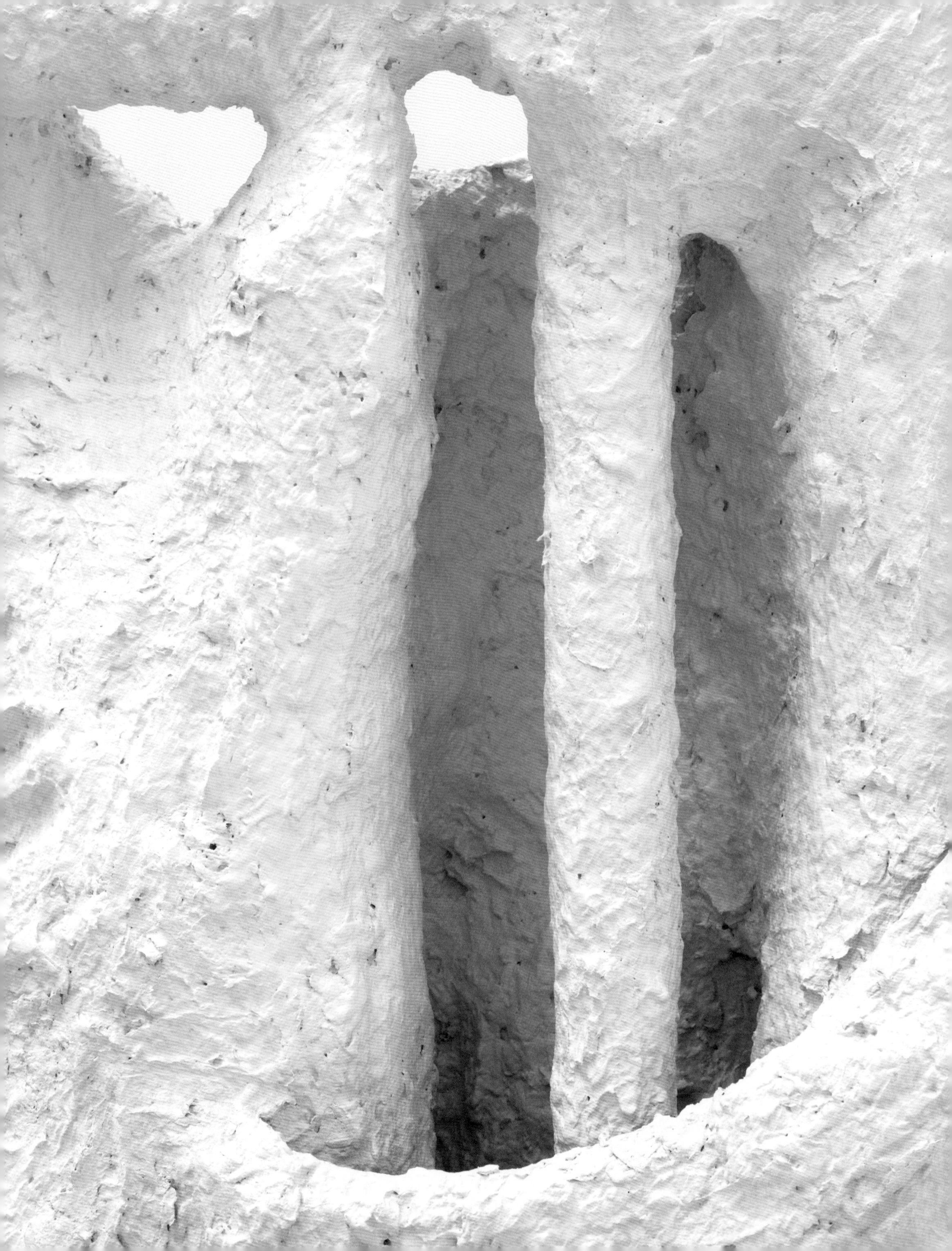

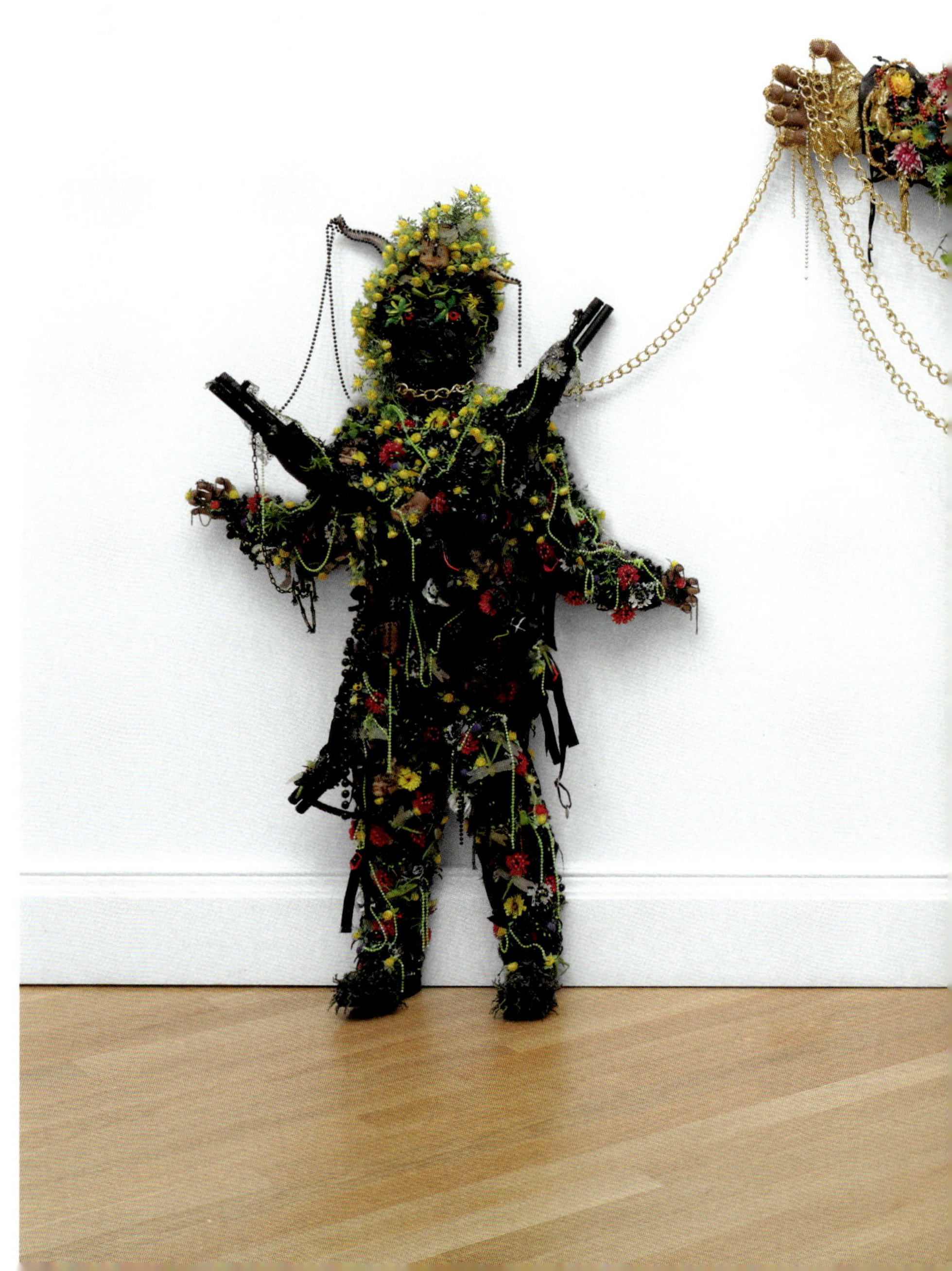

Hew Locke, *The Kingdom of the Blind*
#5 #6 & #7, 2008
Mixed media, 318 × 600 × 36 cm

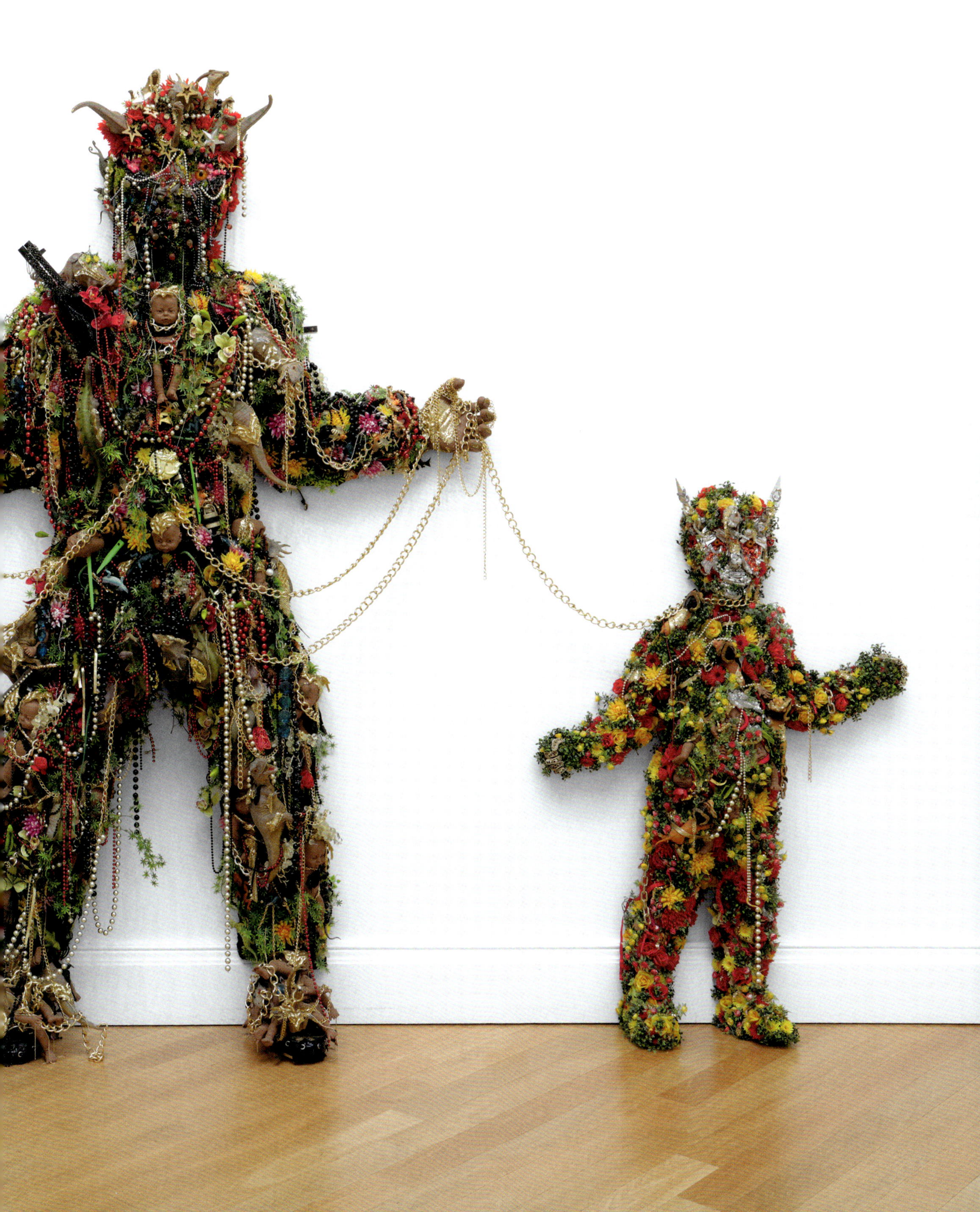

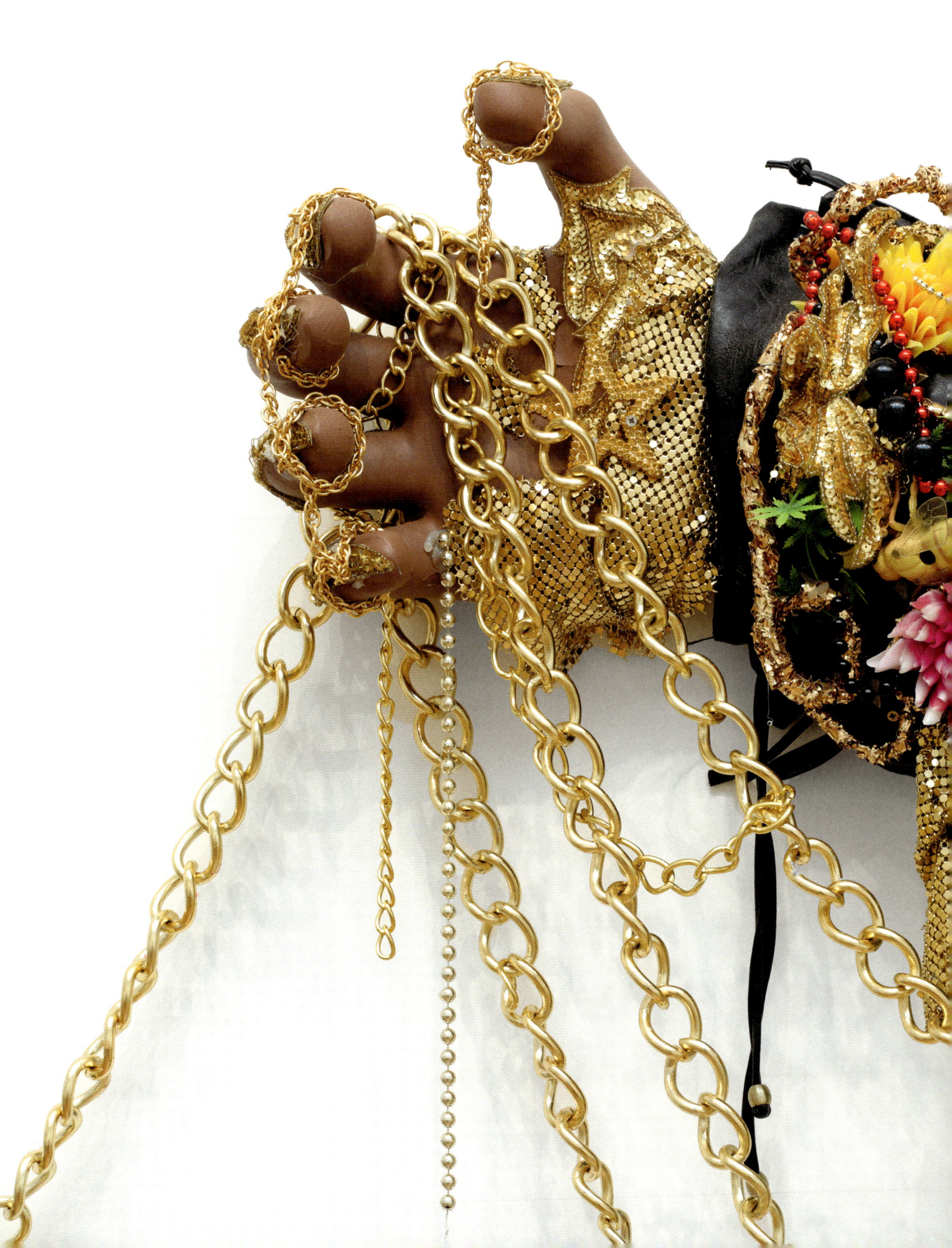

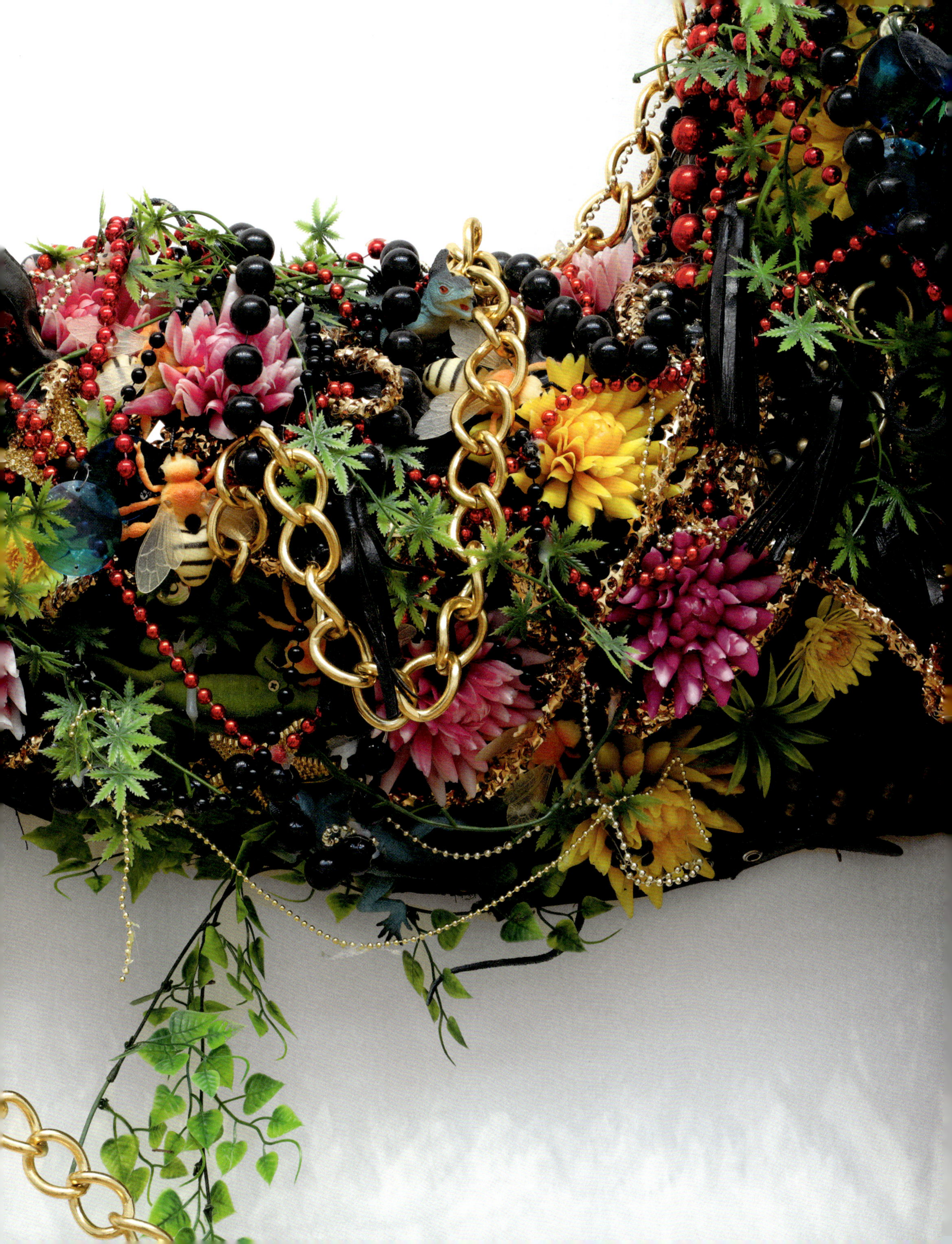

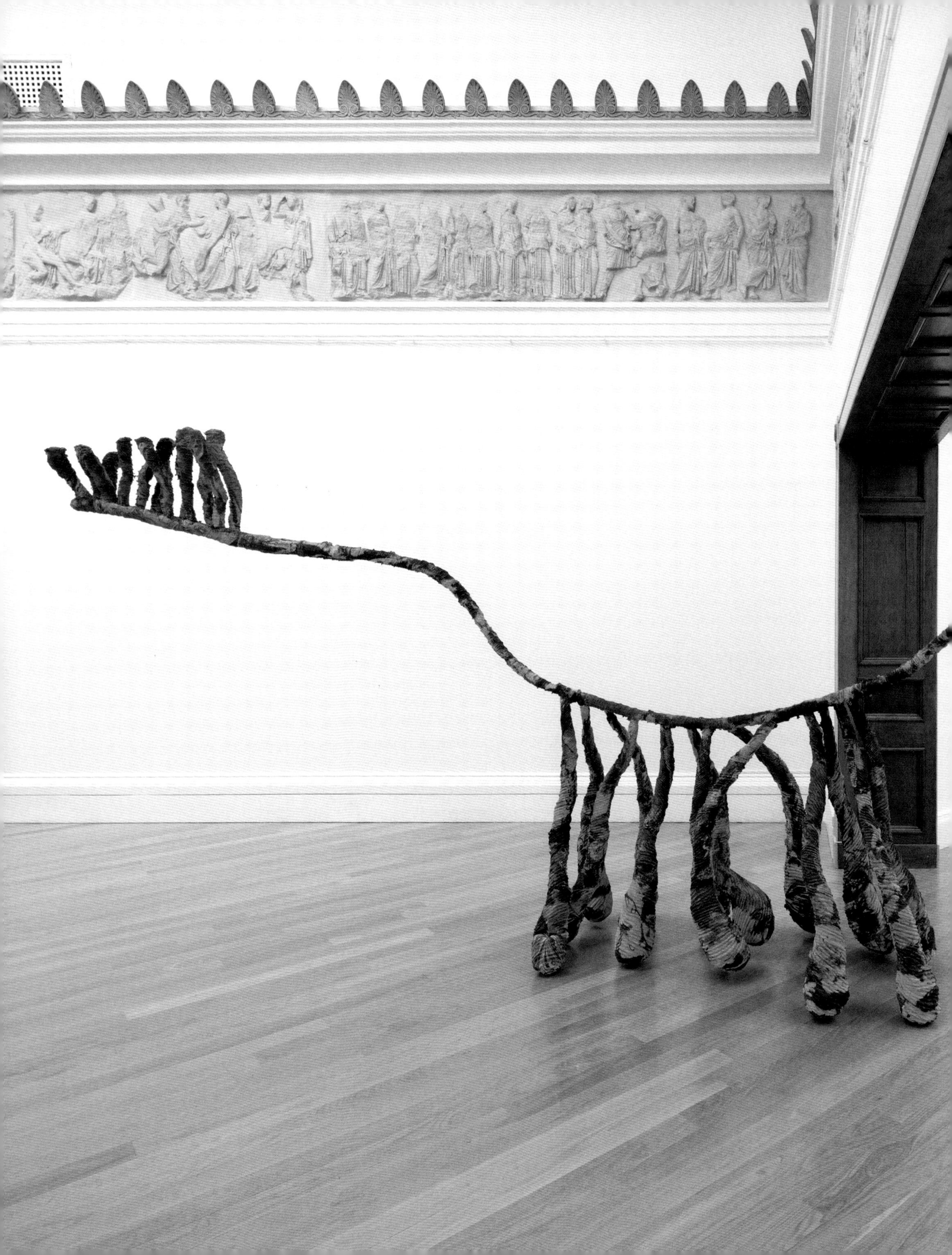

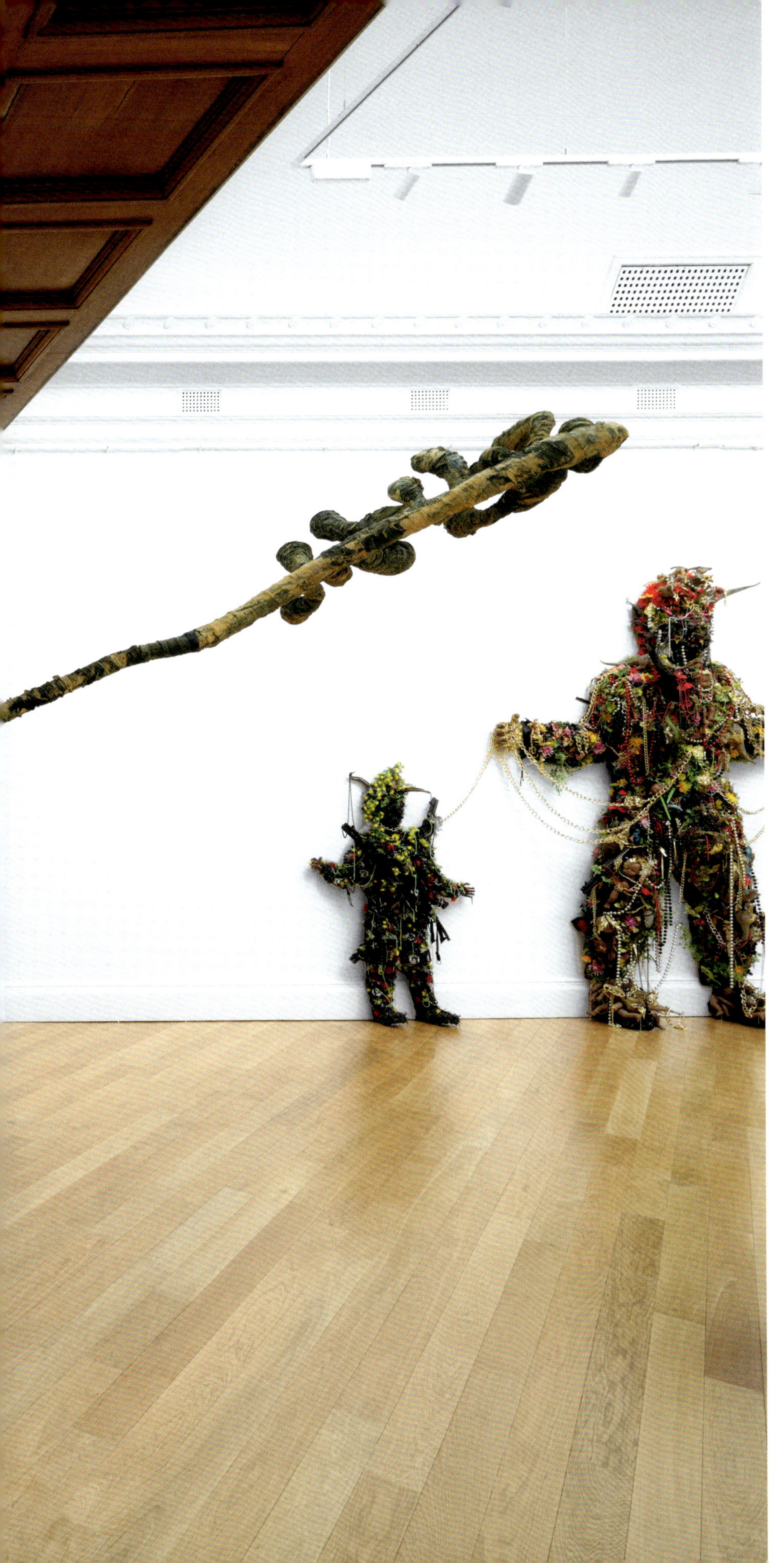

Andrew Sabin, *From Time to Time*, 2018
Pigmented polyurethane and steel,
300 × 800 × 120 cm

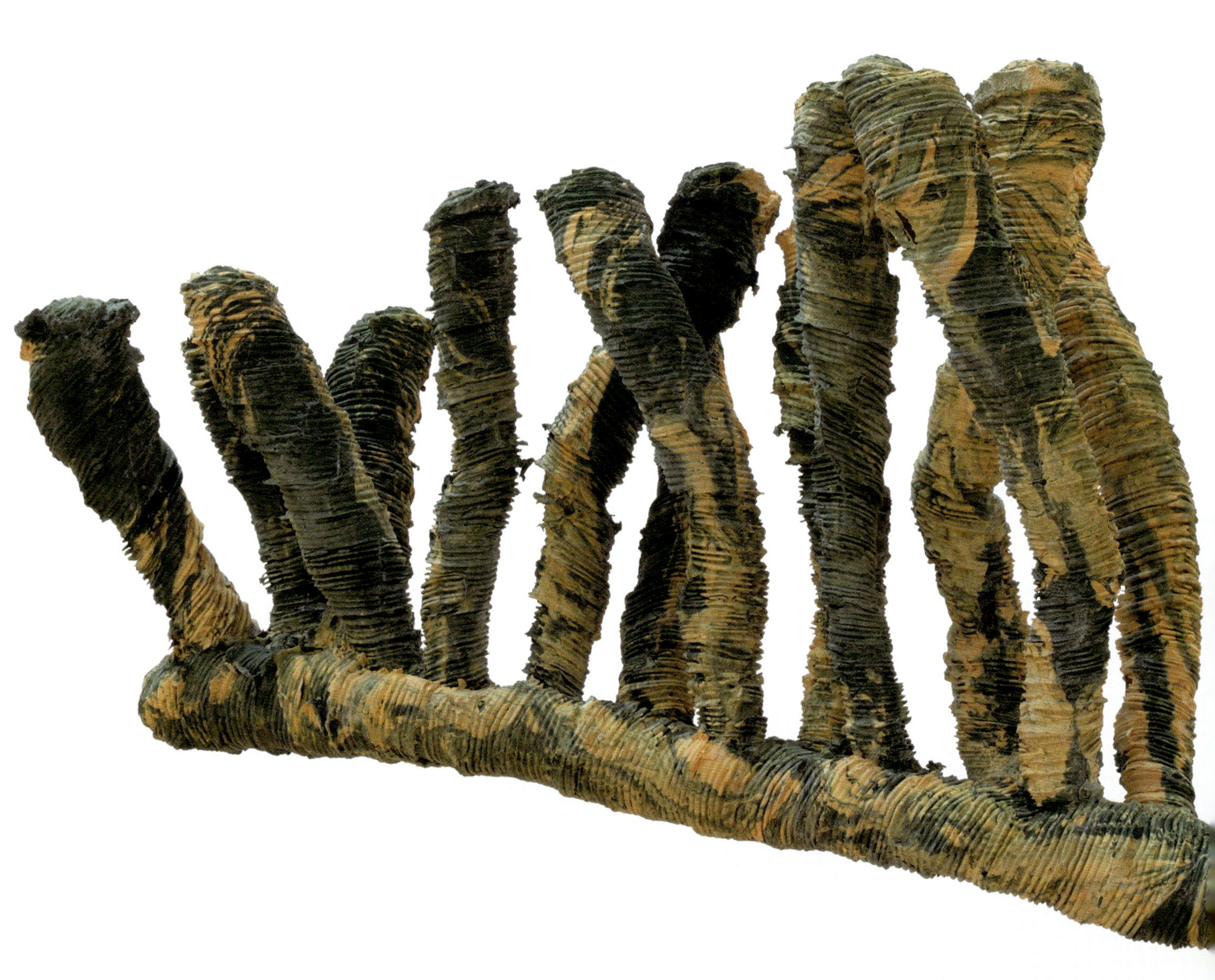

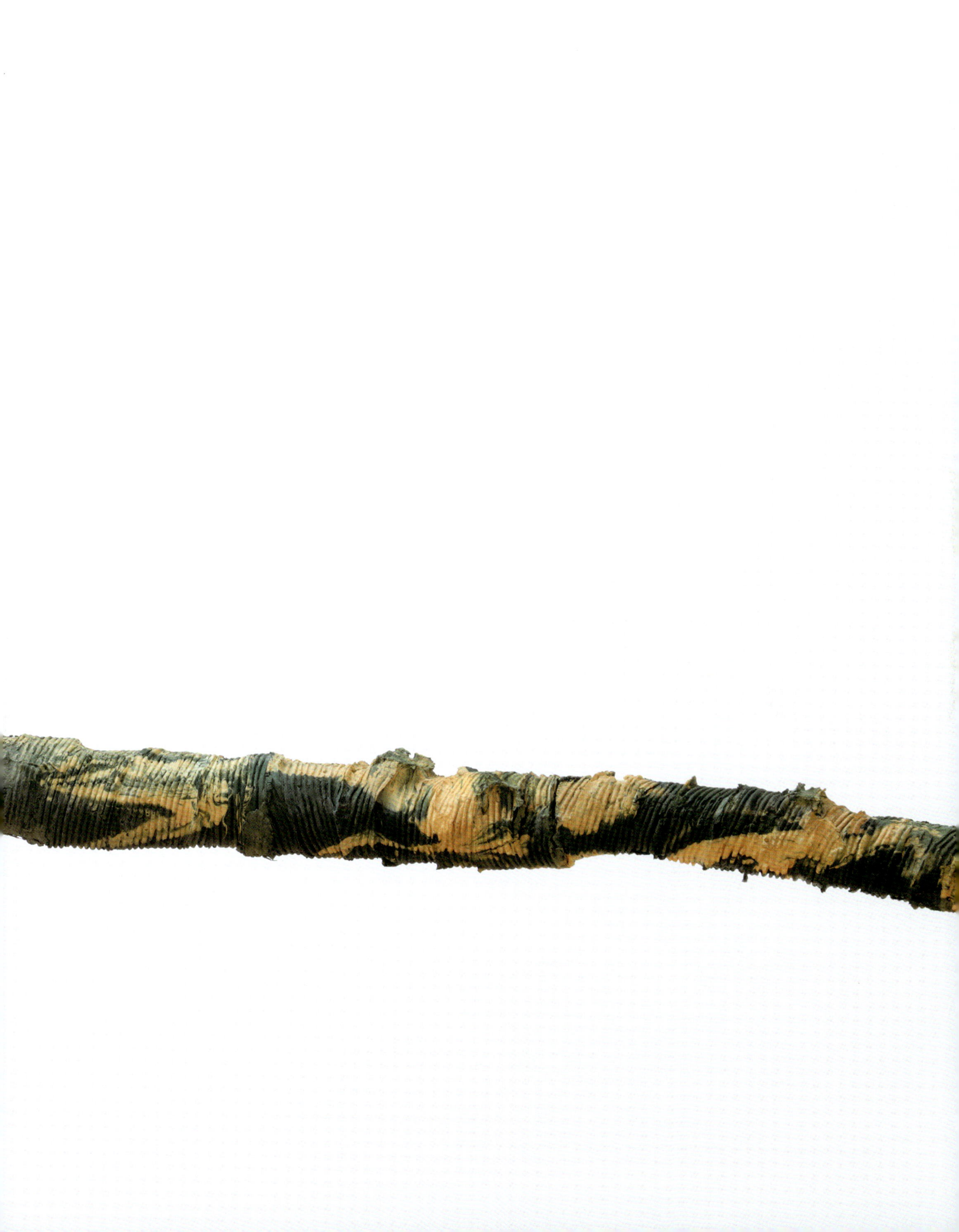

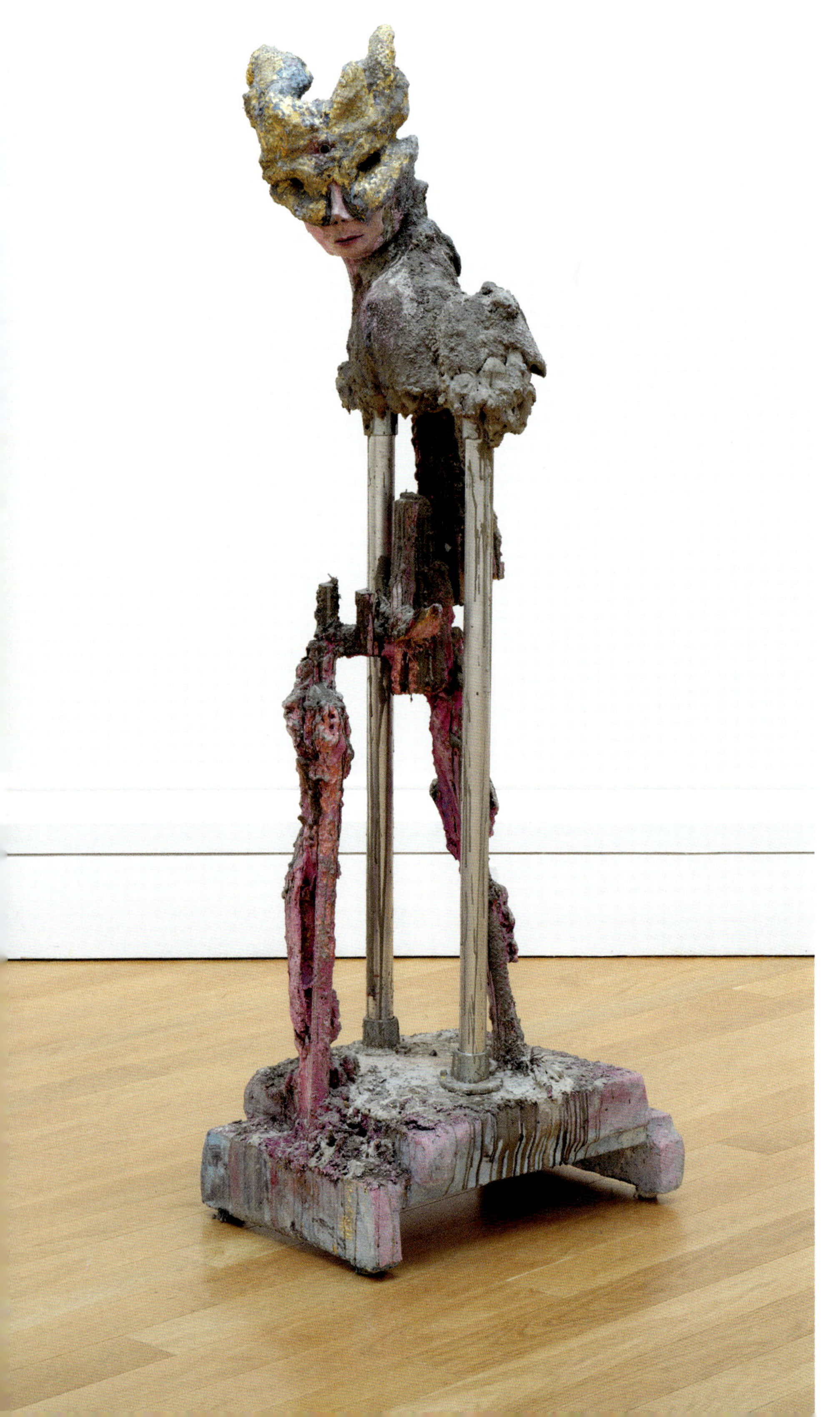

John Summers, *High Ground*, 2023
Wood, plaster, Jesmonite, cement,
foam, self-drying clay, imitation gold leaf,
glass eye, imitation pearls, oil paint,
glitter, UV varnish, bitumen, PVA and
aluminium scaffold poles, 200 × 58 × 73 cm

John Summers, *Mud and Stars,
Gold Head*, 2022
Plaster, Jesmonite, wood, imitation gold
leaf, metallic paints, glass eyes, glitter,
oil paint, soil, PVA, polystyrene, bitumen,
UV varnish, oversized white sock and
self-drying clay, 192 × 80 × 80 cm

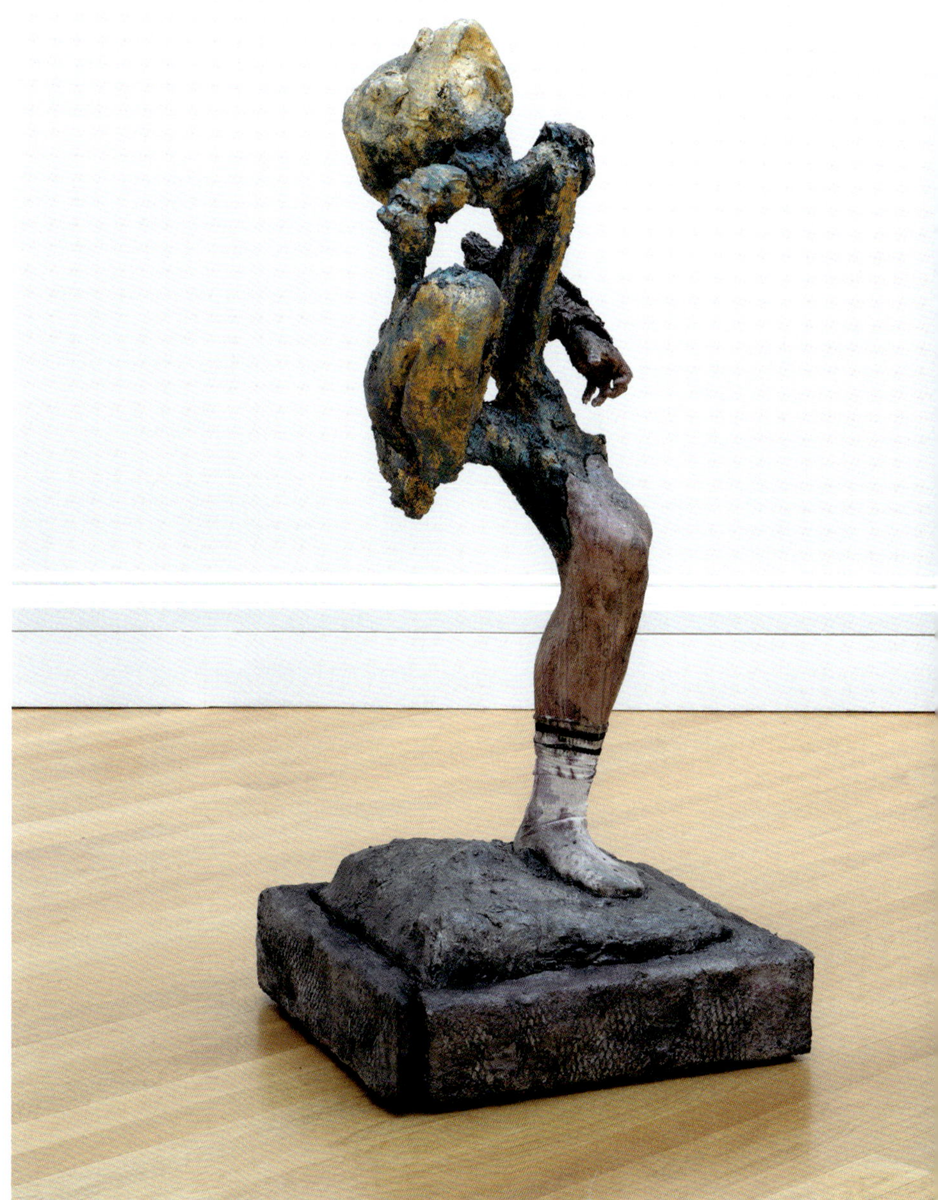

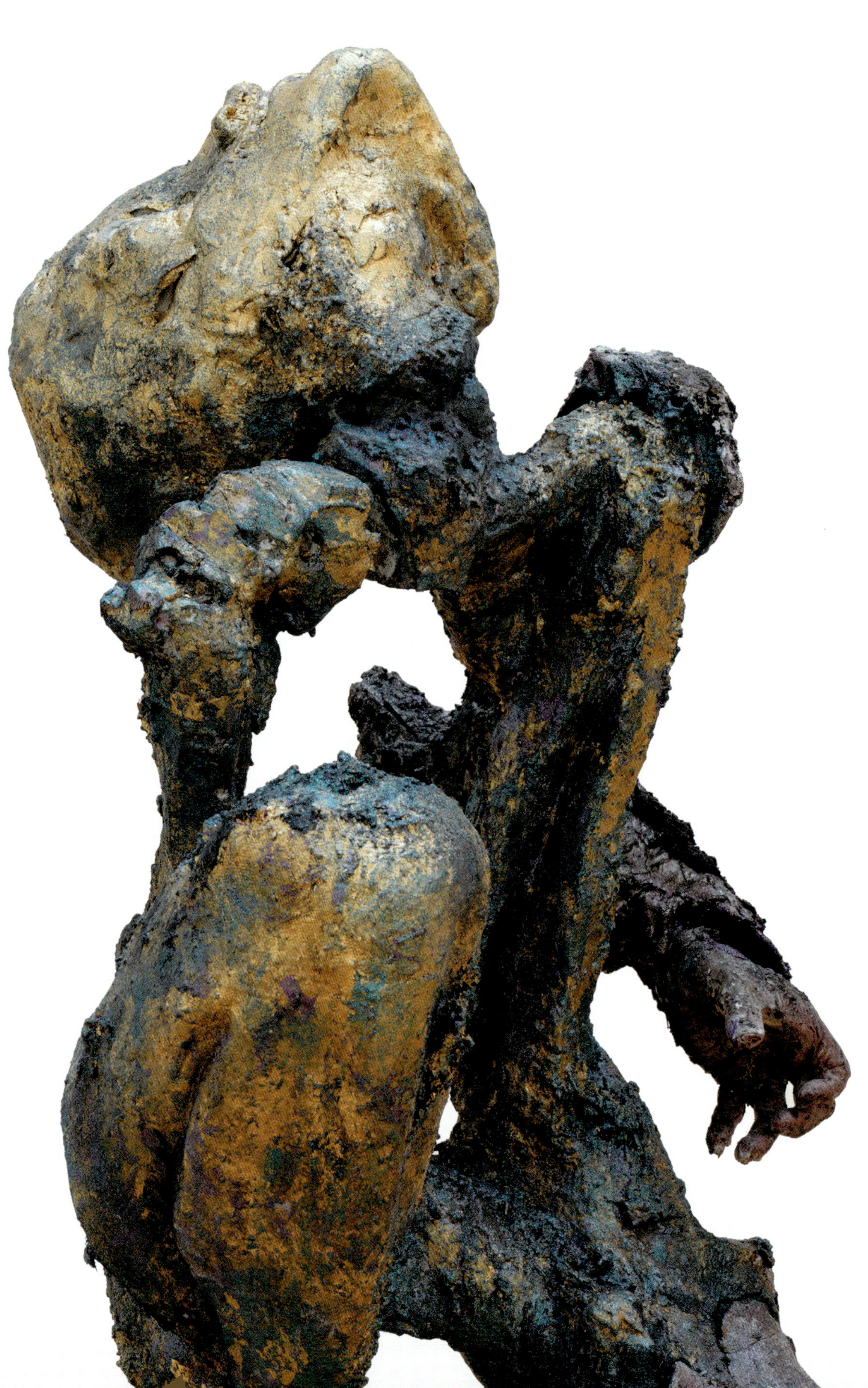

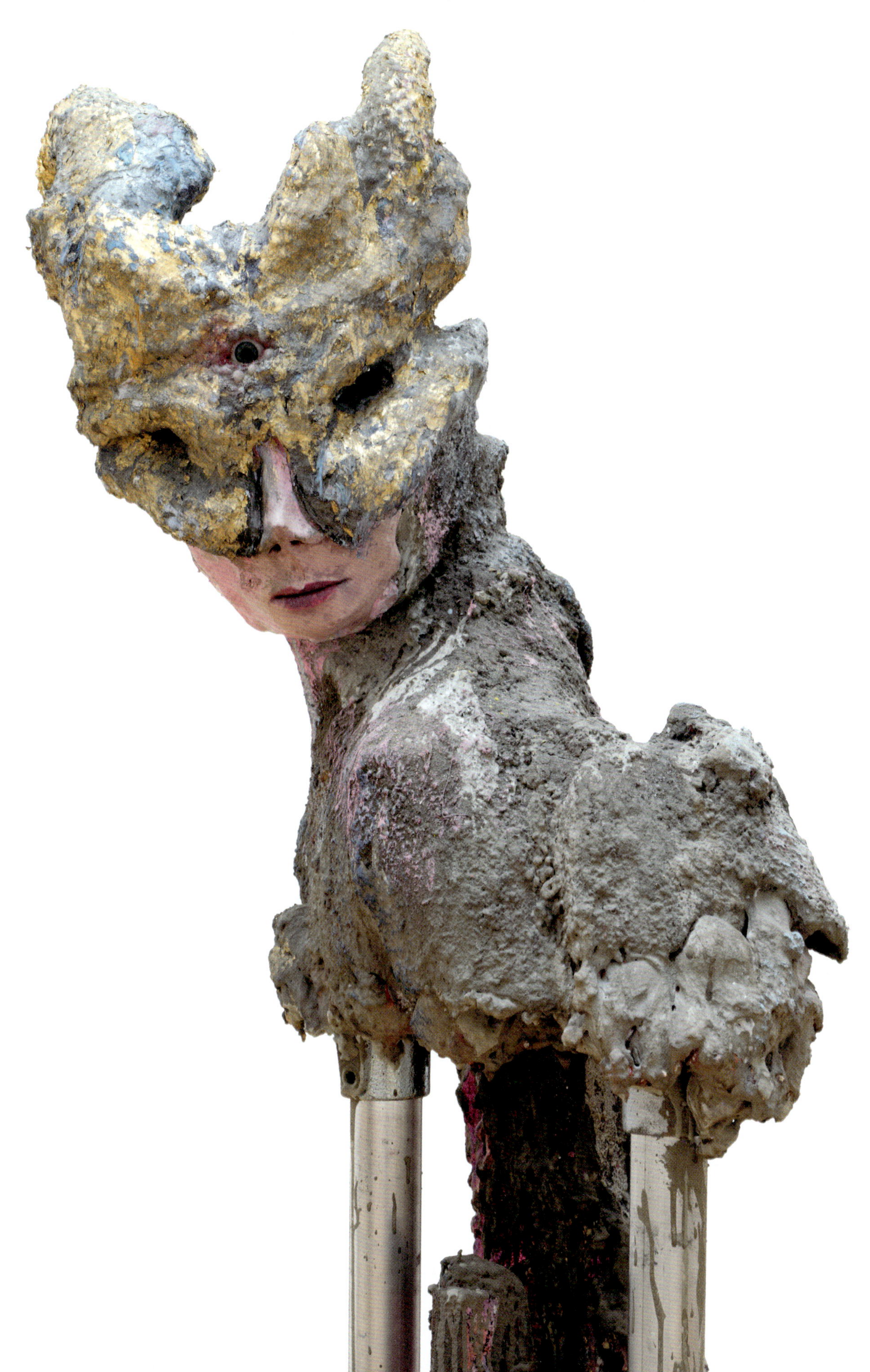

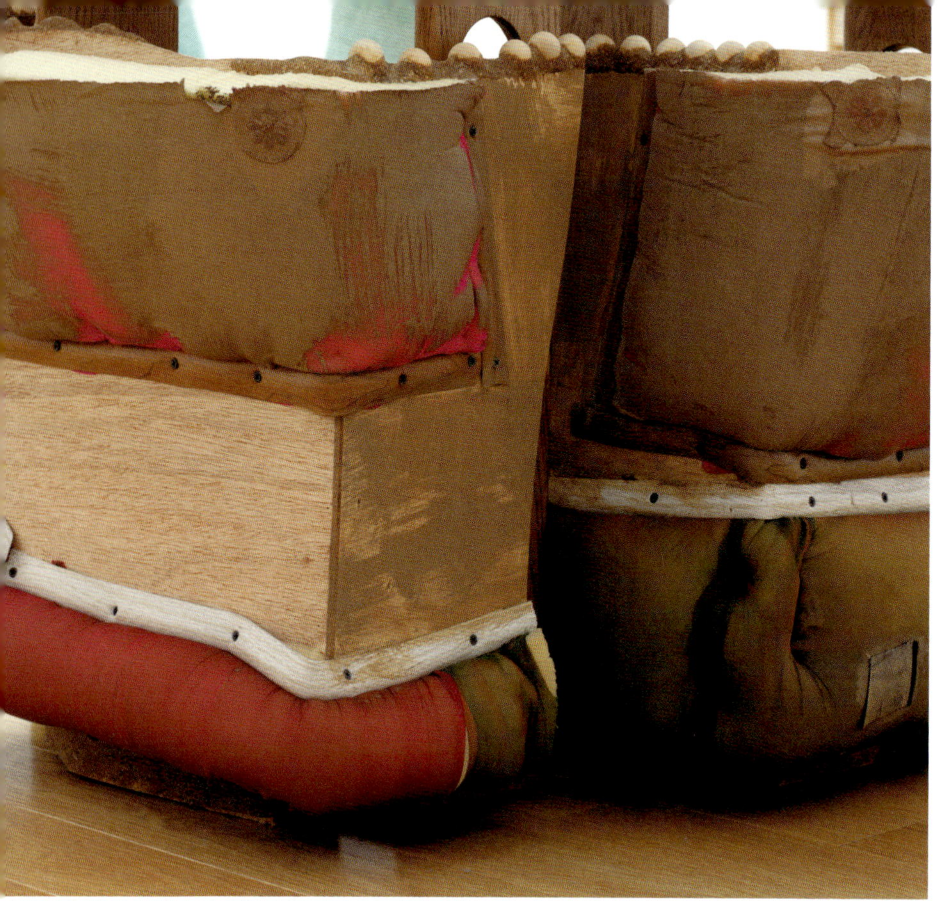

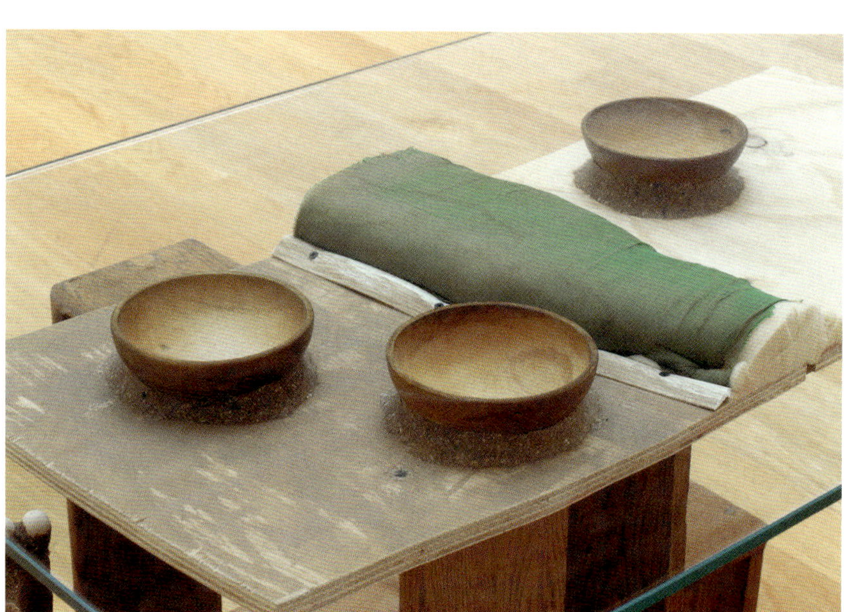

Jessi Reaves, *Three Bowl Table*, 2019
Wood, glass, upholstery foam, paint,
sawdust, wood glue, fabric and hardware,
83.8 × 116.8 × 83.8 cm

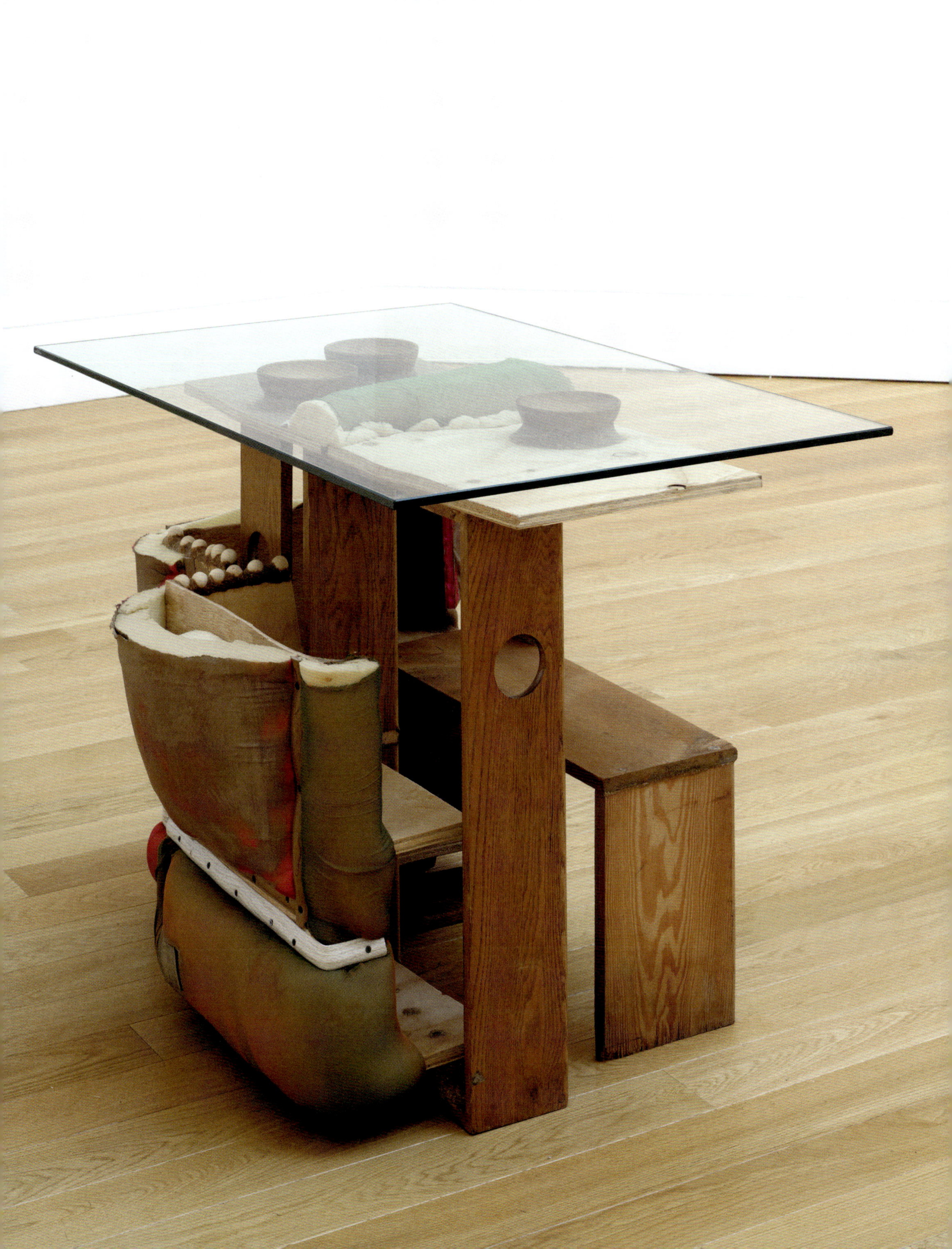

Anna Reading, *Bouquet*, 2022
Metal, plaster, Jesmonite, pigment,
asphalt, oyster shell, black sand,
fishing wire and embroidery thread,
250 × 100 × 90 cm

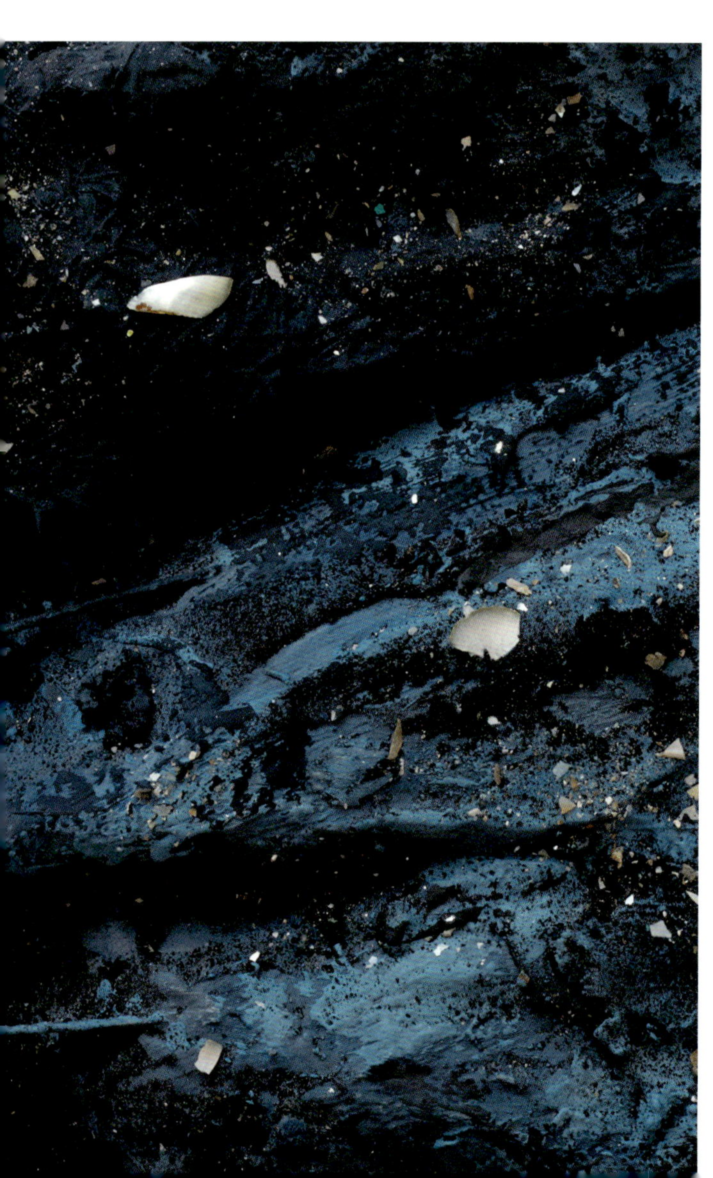

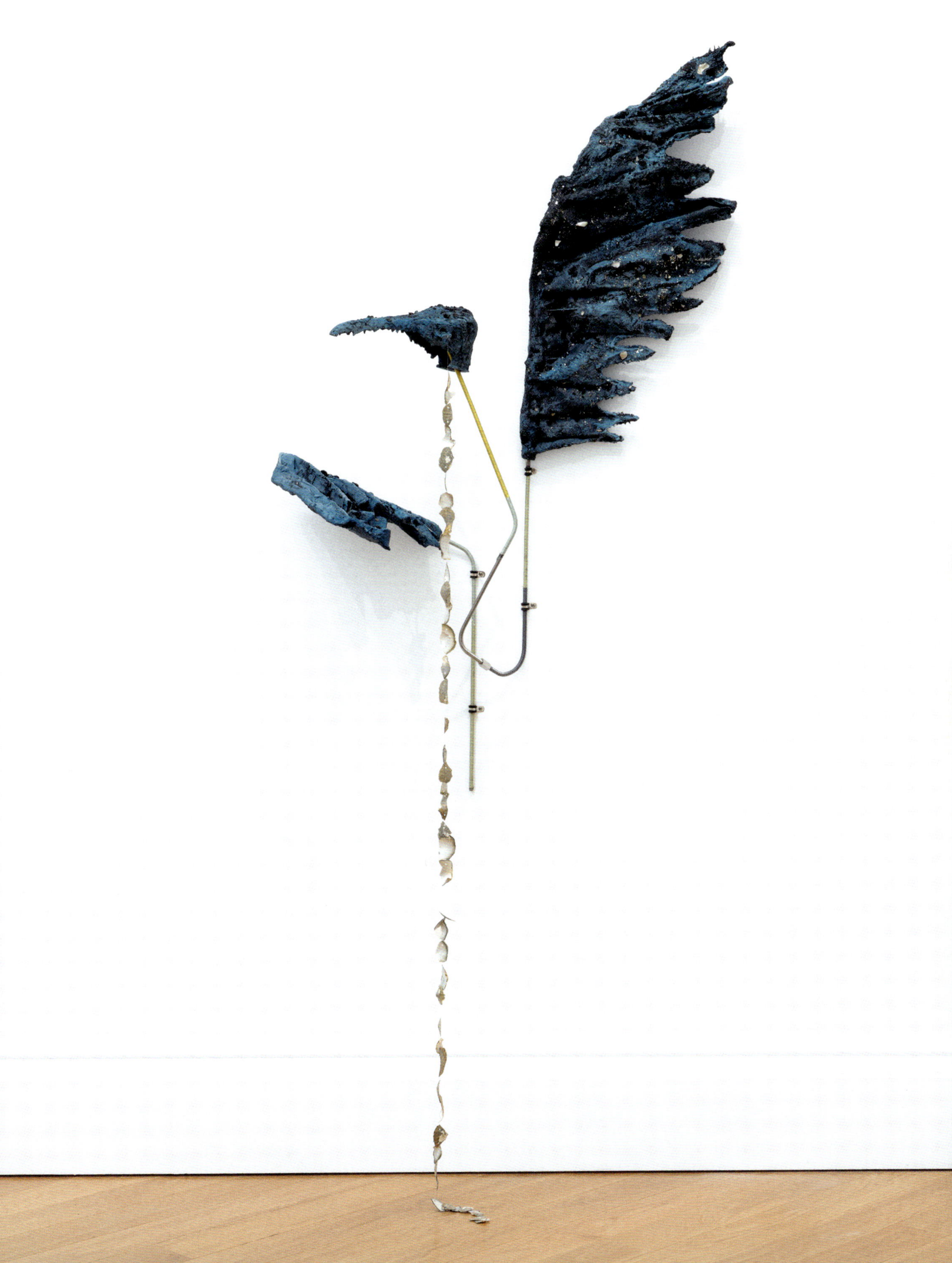

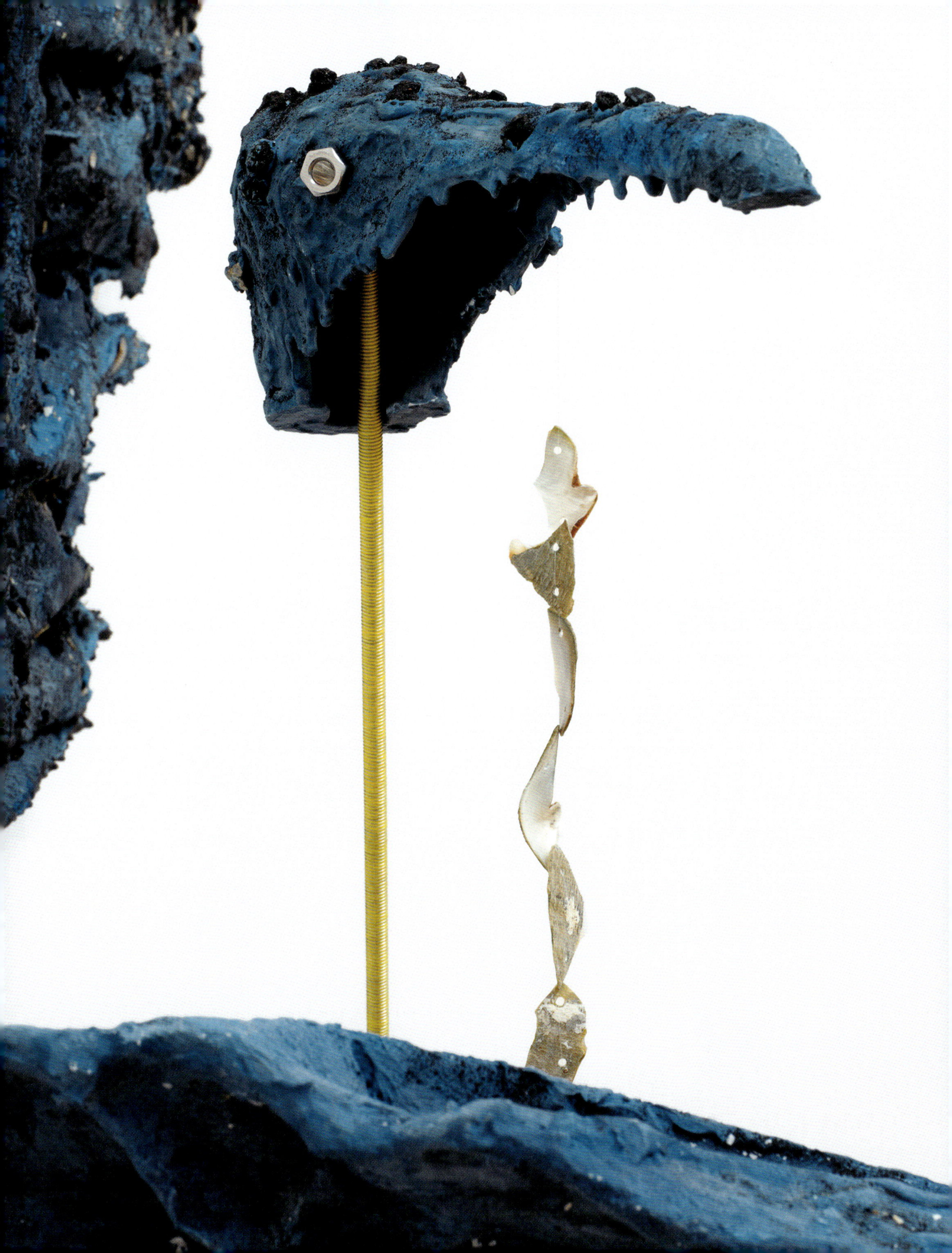

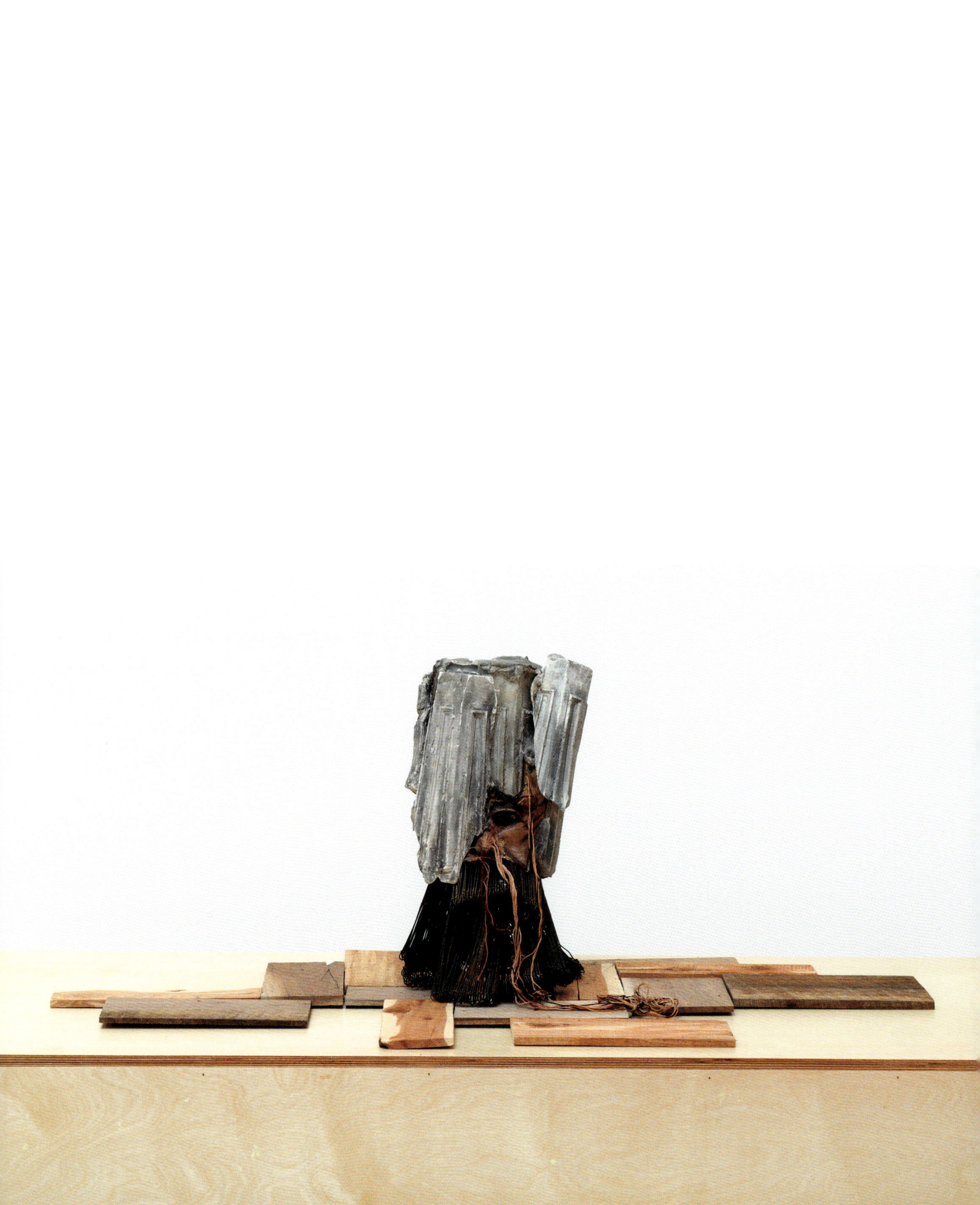

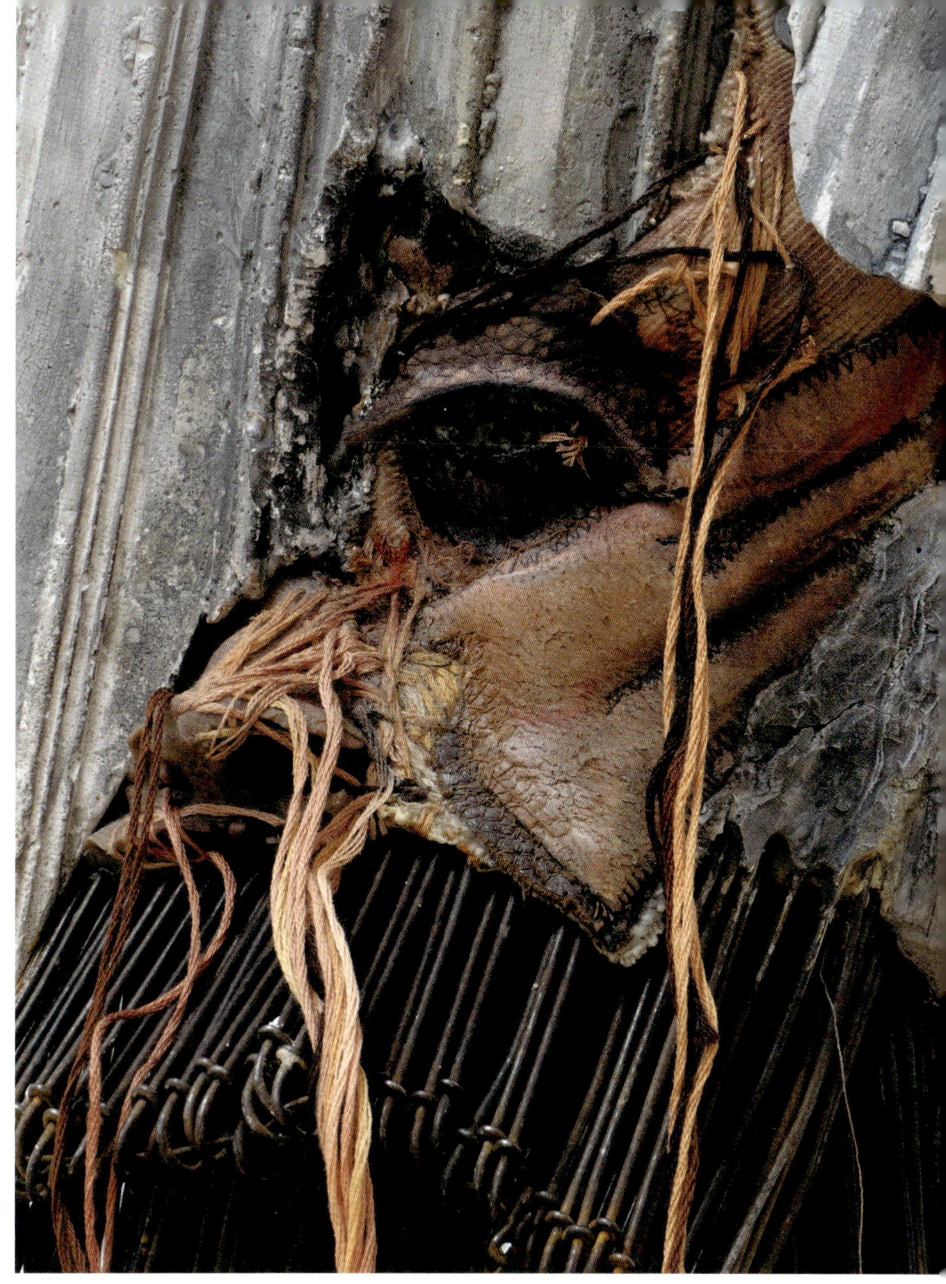

Chiffon Thomas, *Grounded*, 2021
Concrete, silicone, leather, embroidery
floss, rebar wire, pastel, plaster and wood,
53.3 × 125.1 × 69.8 cm

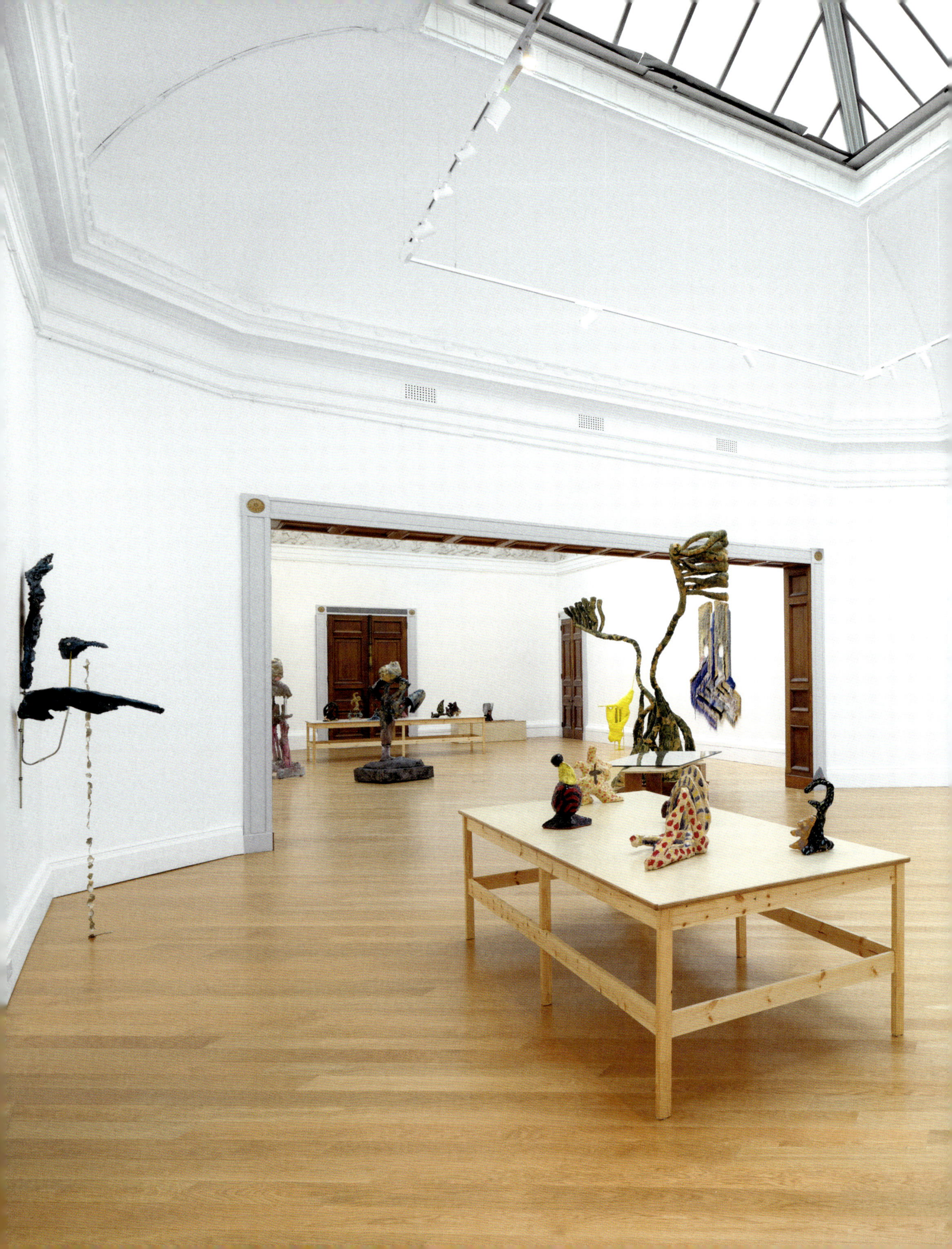

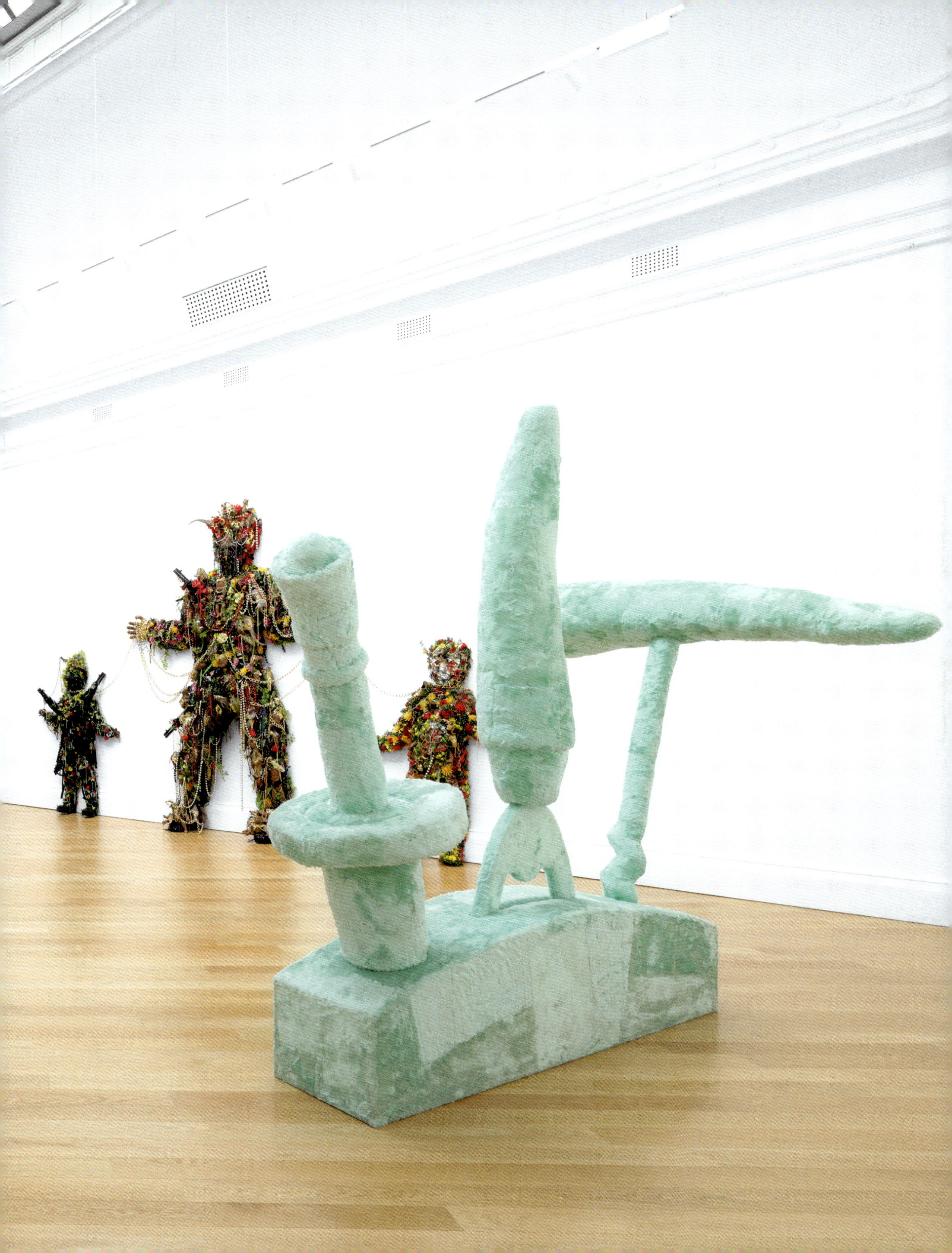

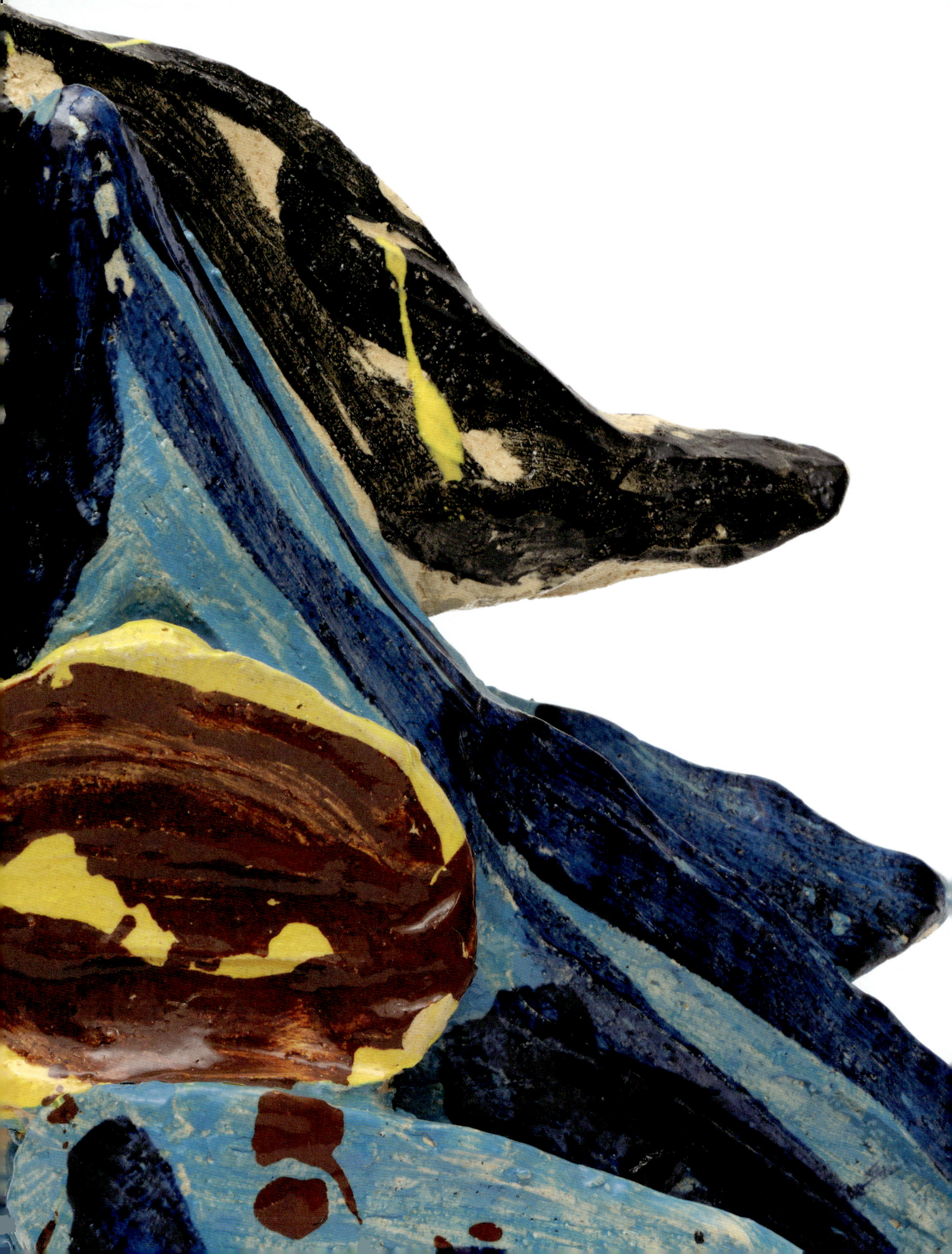

It was Beauty that Killed the Beast

James Fisher

They shot him down…

James Fisher and King Kong have met to see an exhibition of sculpture together. As well as wishing to discuss the sculpture, Kong has brought along a recording of a 1983 Daniel Johnston song about him, *King Kong*, that he has just rediscovered.

KK   Have you heard this? It's like a lament – it reminded me of myself, my constitution and why I wanted to show you these sculptures.

They shot him down…

JF   Well, you're a kind of hybrid, aren't you? A man in a gorilla costume.
KK   Yes, but I am also part man, part Godzilla; part Willis O'Brien, part mechanical model. I thought I would recognise myself in these things; they're part one thing, part another-ness. I saw another hybridity exhibition a few years back, which I very much enjoyed. You know, since I have become something of an exhibit – a sideshow – myself, I more often look to exhibitions to try to find out how I belong in this world. They've chained me up in a theatre, and they bring people to look at me, but I am watching them back, and I am slowly piecing together what it is that they find so captivating.

They thought he was a monster…

JF   So, did that hybridity exhibition give you any answers?
KK   Well, not directly, but I will come to that. You see, to begin with, being an *attraction* was disorientating. I was already a bit unsettled by the temporal disruption: one minute I am fighting an *Elasmosaurus*, the next I am in a theatre on Broadway. Also, Merian had always called me Komodo and said I was *King of the Komodo*, but I look nothing like a dragon.
JF   He wanted you to be Godzilla?
KK   I don't know. I mean, I might be a lizard, but I think there is too much primate, too much Willis and too much Merian in me for that. When people came to see me early on, I thought they saw a monster. There seemed to be a mixture of fear and awe in their eyes. But as more visitors queued to see me, and I watched more carefully, I realised that what I was perceiving was incredulity. *And they were laughing at me.*

But he was the king…

JF   Really? Why do you think that was?
KK   Well, I suppose that was what I was trying to find out at that other hybridity exhibition. I got the sense that it might have something to do with the part one thing, part another. There were objects that were both woman and dolphin, for example, or simultaneously landscape and robot. I kept expecting to see myself, only for the recognition to slip away. Something was always withheld, and I think this was because they were all made of bronze. The bronze casting had a homogenising effect, like a veil. It's as if it is not enough to be an amalgam of things: what my sightseers see in me, and what they find funny, is the *process* of becoming. The recognition of themselves transforming into something other.

And they tied him
And they took him across the ocean…

JF   Is this why you've brought me to this exhibition? To witness a transformation?

KK   I think so. I've been thinking about a television series called *Manimal*, which coincidentally was made in the same year as this Daniel Johnston record. I visited Stan Winston's studio…

JF   I remember *Manimal*! There was a boy in my class at school who gained playground kudos from his interpretation of a pulsating human hand transforming into a panther paw.

KK   That's funny, because Stan said that while the premise was that Jonathan Chase could turn himself into any creature, *Manimal* had such a small budget that most of the stories involved him transforming into either a hawk or a panther. Anyway, at the studio, Stan showed me the meticulous special effects process for the panther transformation. He made a sequence of models of Chase's head, each with an incremental shape-shift to panther.

And they chained him
And put him in the show…

JF   This is all fascinating, but what does it have to do with the sculptures we are looking at here?

KK   I obviously haven't explained myself very well. Stan's models were arranged in the studio in order. The models at each end weren't remarkably interesting, but those in between made me laugh. In their sheer viscerality, I saw myself. I saw my humanness in a moment of transition into something else. When I brought you to see these sculptures, this is what I hoped to show you.

JF   A moment of transition?

KK   Well, yes. But not just of ideas. I am sure I recognise myself here: it's in the *materiality* of how the shape-shift is articulated. Part some stuff, part other stuff. Look at this thing. It is earth and dirt and glass and tar, but it is also human. One of its legs is dissolving, or is it emerging? All I know is that when I look back it will be another thing at another stage.

JF   I once watched a pink-toed tarantula moulting. It looked comical and awkward.

KK   That's sort of it, but what I am apprehending is an instant, hovering between the primate – the human – and the bestial or the carnal. It is held in its substance, and it is beautiful because it tells me what I didn't want to hear.

'Twas beauty
That killed the beast…

James Fisher (b.1972) lives and works in Gloucestershire; he is represented by Eagle Gallery, London. He was awarded a PhD in Fine Art at the University of Gloucestershire in 2009. Fisher's paintings are held in many private and public collections in the UK, Europe and USA.

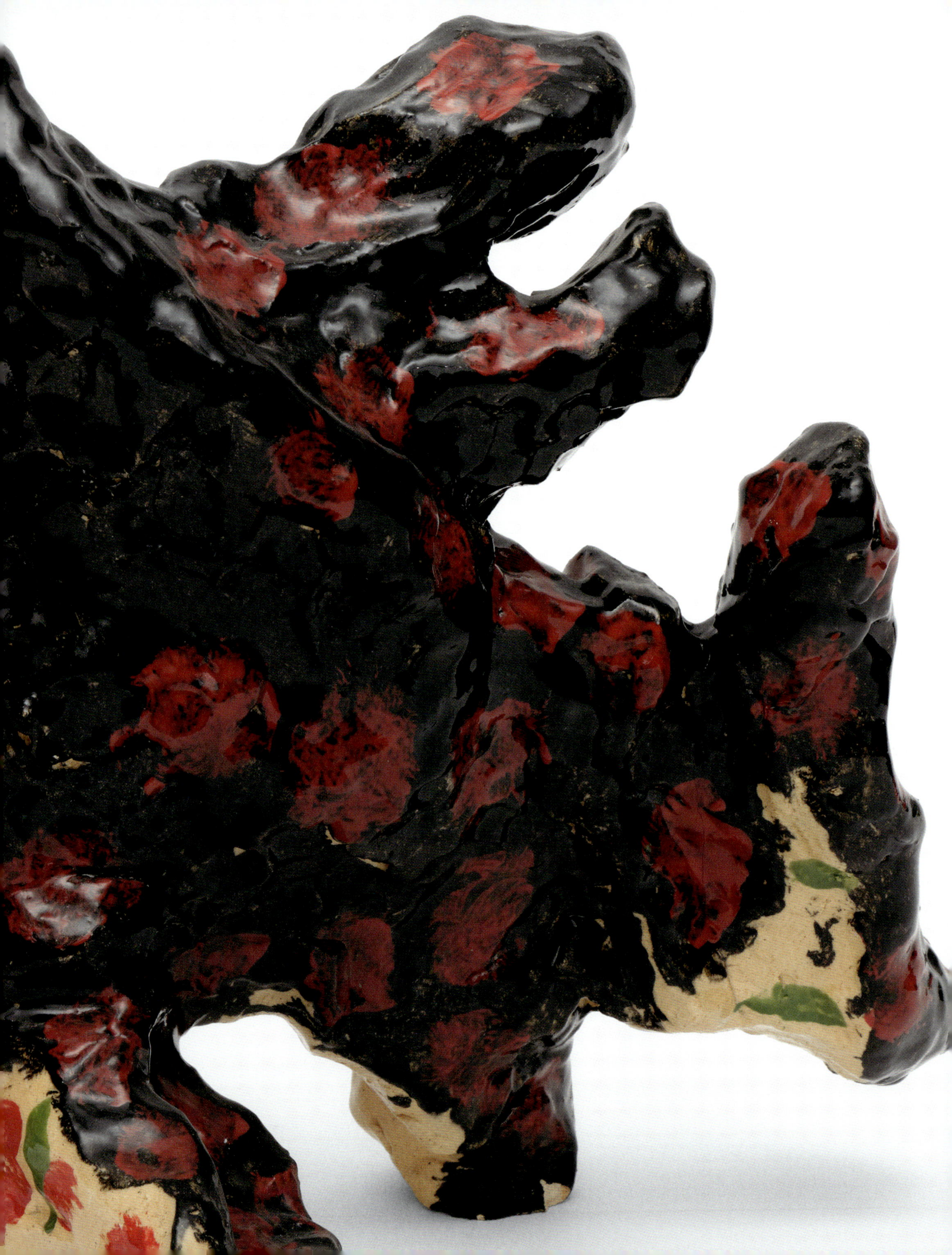

Shifting Surfaces: Selections from John Hoyland's Photographic Archive

Hannah Hughes

Motion blurs, light trails
flares, refractions
ricocheting flash
migrations from the photographic surface

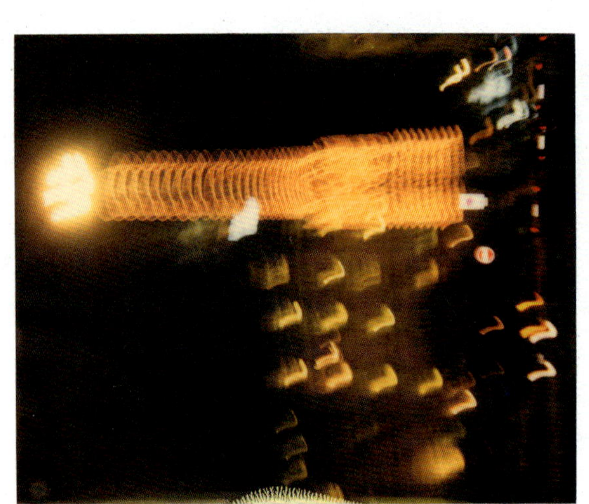

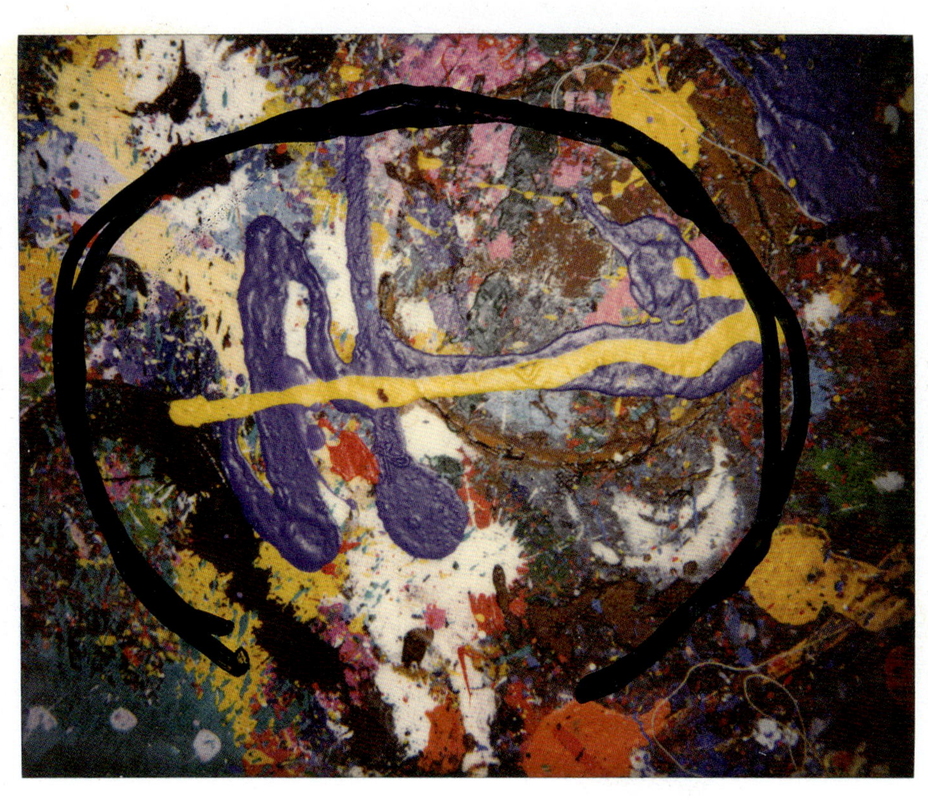

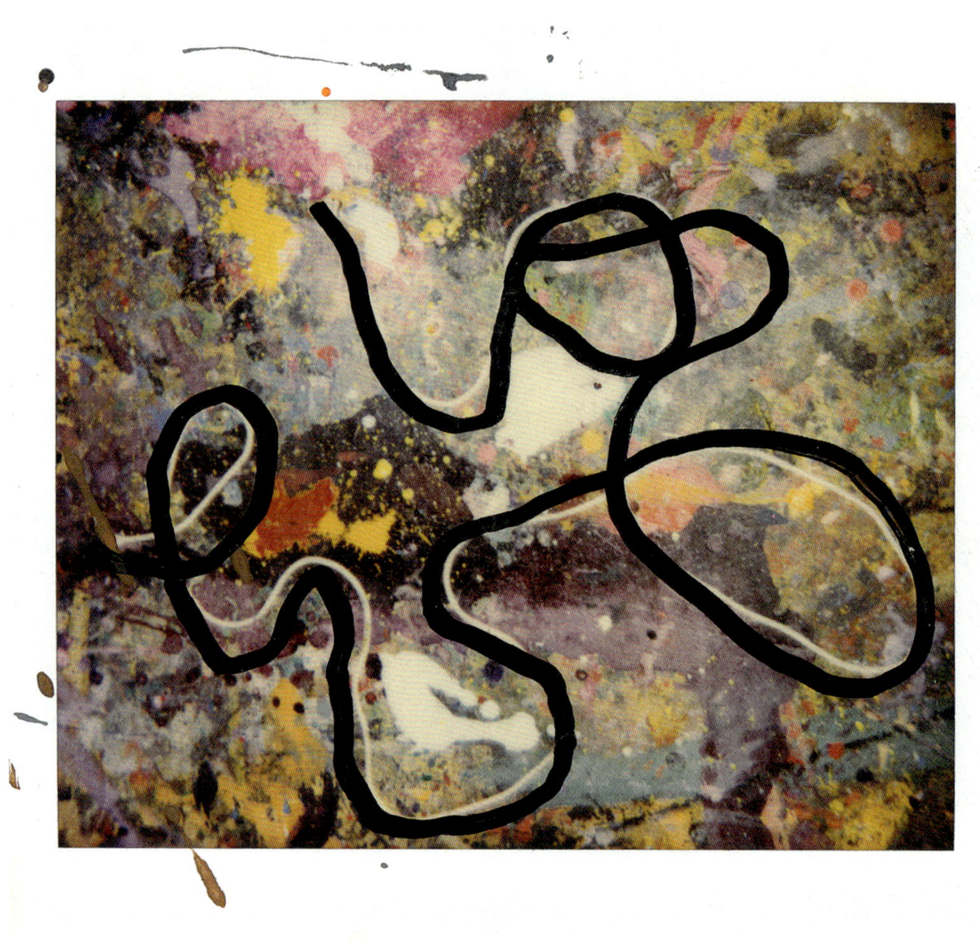

Found marks
drips, splatters
stains, spills
skins, crusts

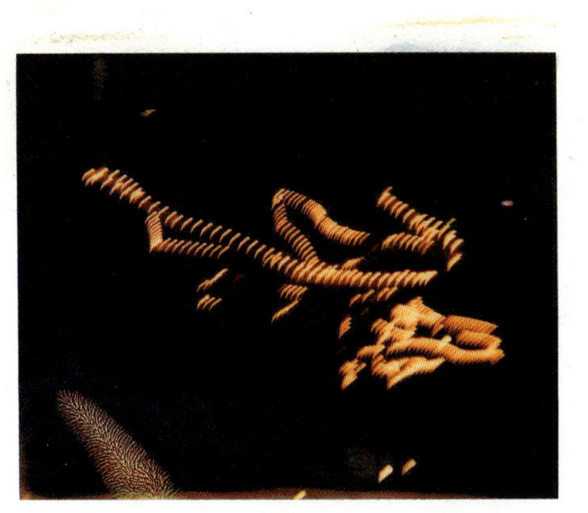

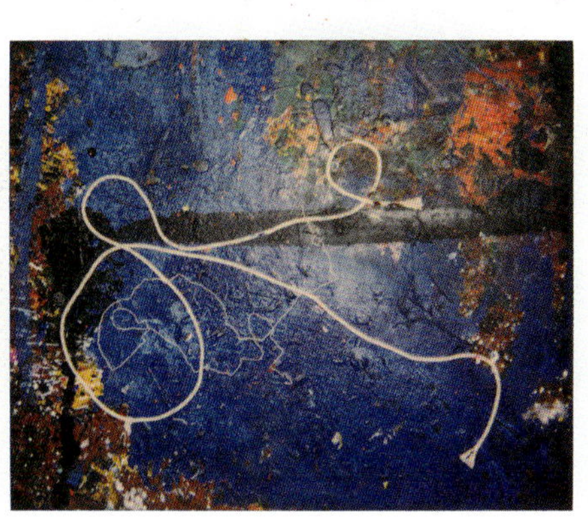

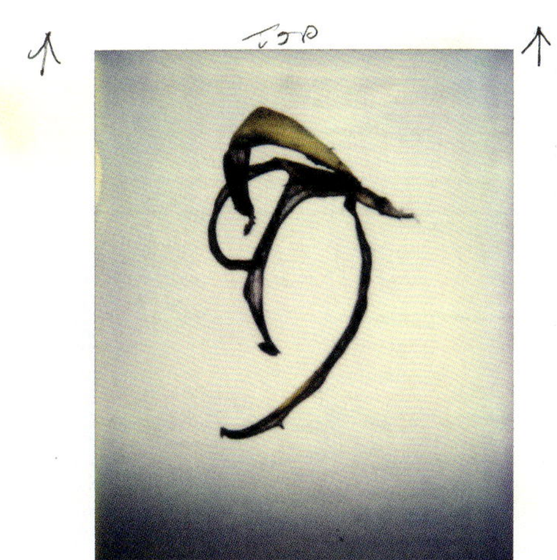

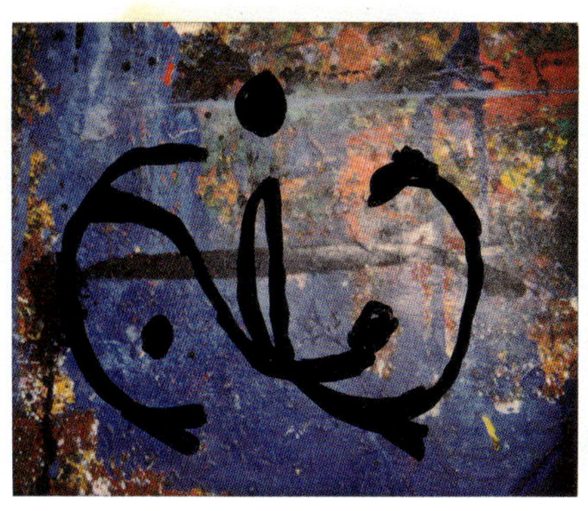

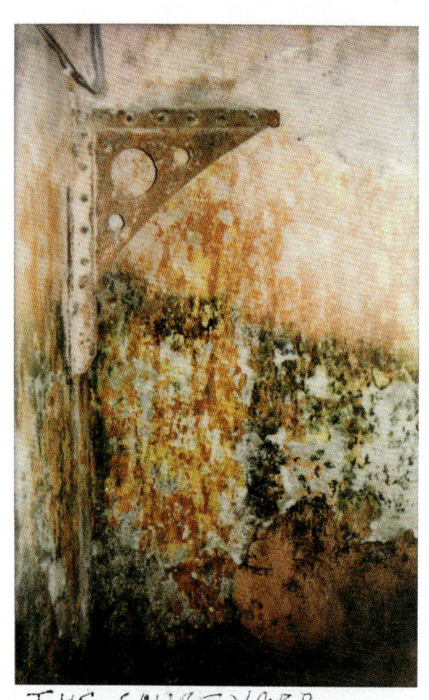

THE COURTYARD

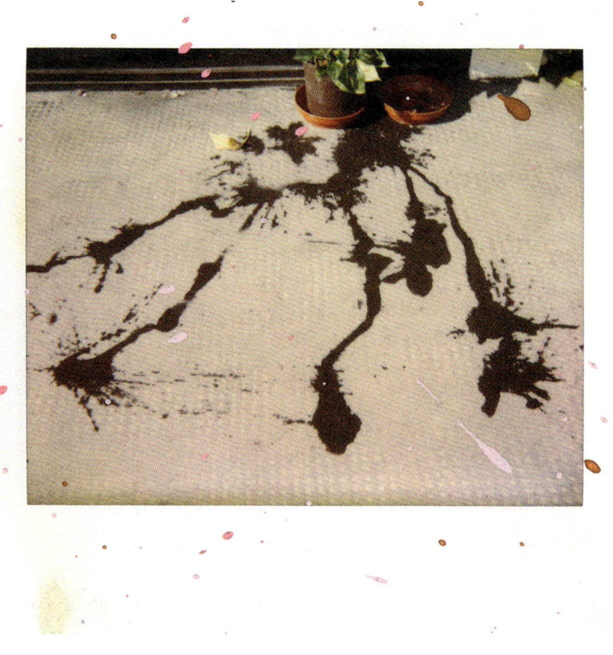

Disturbed surfaces
flaws and chemical reactions
erosions of photographic emulsion
fingerprint erasures

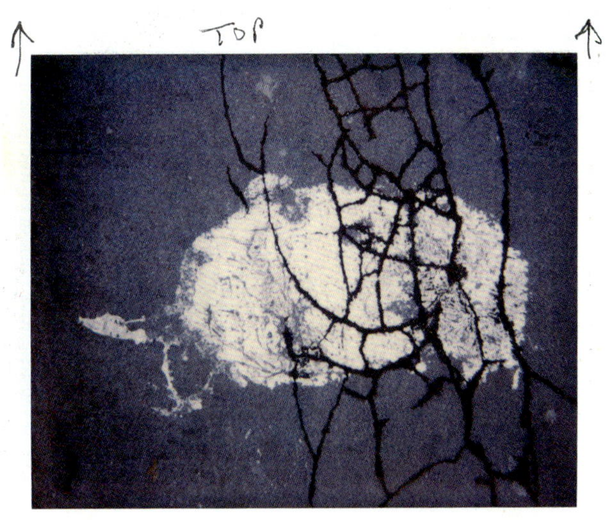

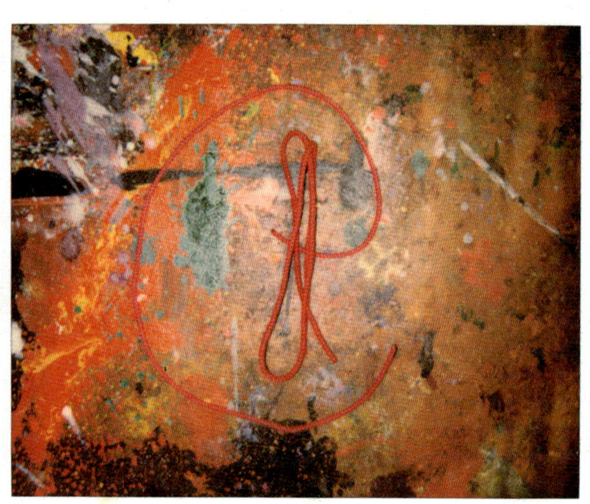 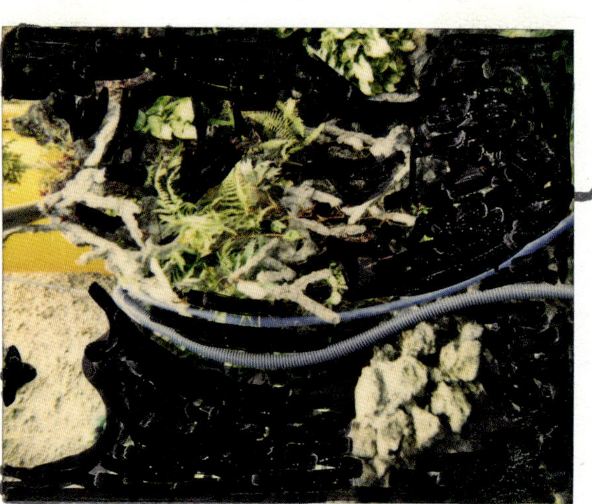

OTB

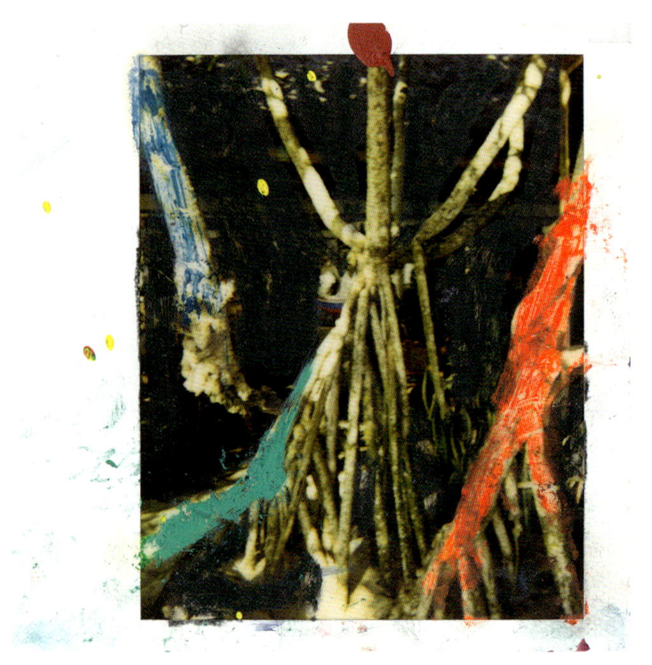 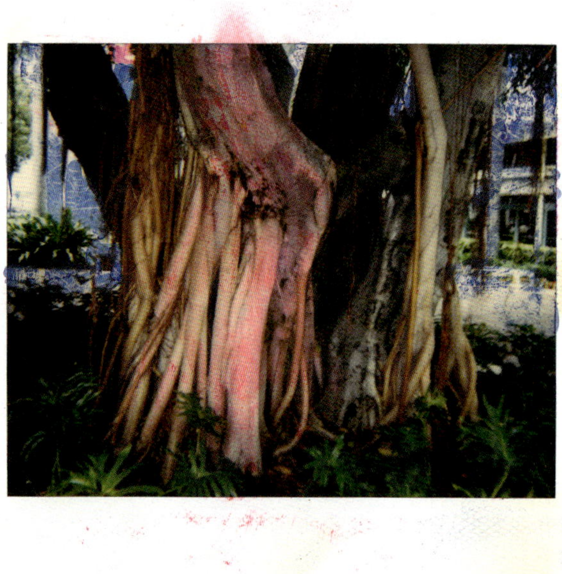

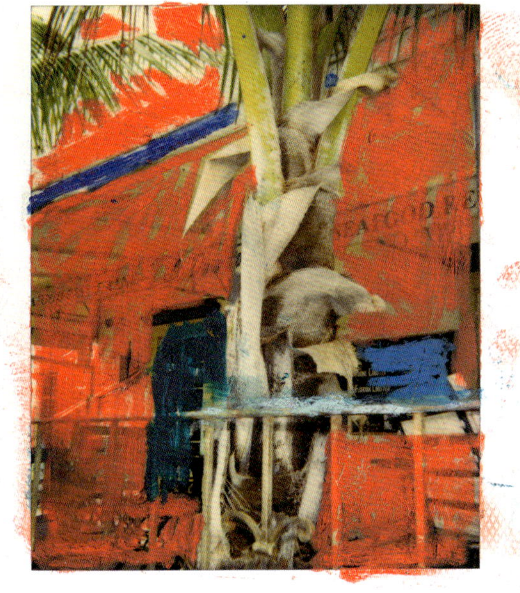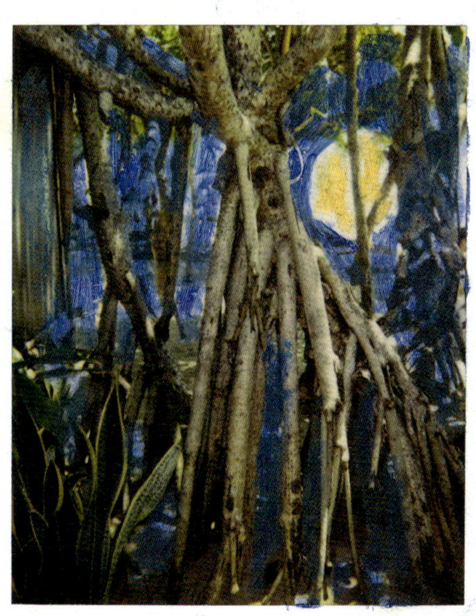

Hannah Hughes (b.1975) is a London-based artist. She graduated from the University of Brighton in 1997 and her work has since been exhibited internationally. She is currently a PhD candidate at the University of Gloucestershire.

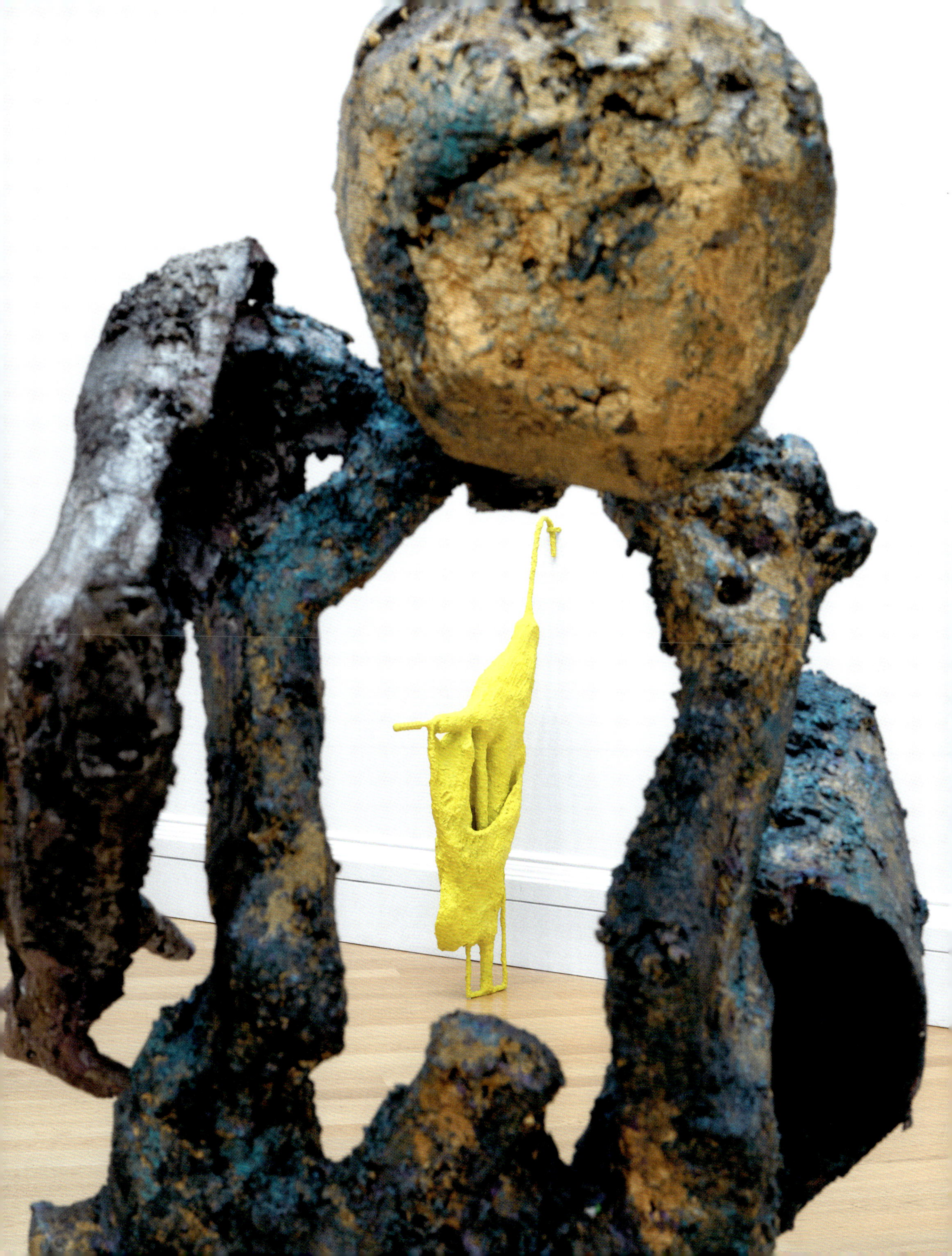

Caroline Achaintre (Toulouse, France, b.1969) was raised in Germany and now lives and works in the UK. She attended the Kunsthochschule in Halle, Chelsea College of Art and Design, and Goldsmiths, University of London. Achaintre draws from multiple and radically different cultural references. With her sculptures made of wool, her ceramics and her watercolour drawings, she appropriates each space to install her hybrid creatures, transforming the exhibition venue into a theatre where a dialogue between different characters half-fantastic, half-ghostly can take place. Her work is held in numerous public collections, including: Centre Pompidou, Paris; CAPC, Bordeaux; Tate Britain, London; Musée d'Art Moderne de la Ville de Paris, Paris; Arts Council Collection, UK; Centre national des arts plastiques, Paris; FRAC Aquitaine, Bordeaux; and FRAC Champagne-Ardenne, Reims.

Eric Bainbridge (Consett, UK, b.1955) is a British sculptor who came to prominence in the 1980s with solo shows at the Walker Art Center in Minneapolis, the Stedelijk Museum in Amsterdam and the AIR Gallery in London. He exhibited in two Venice Biennales, and was represented by Salvatore Ala (1985–2014). Recent exhibitions include: *Aftermeiter/Lodgers*, Haus Modrath, Cologne (2017–18); *Poor Things*, Fruitmarket, Edinburgh (2023); and *PLUCKPLUCK*, Workplace, London (2023).

Phyllida Barlow (Newcastle upon Tyne, UK, b.1944 – London, UK, d.2023) took inspiration from her surroundings to create imposing installations that can be at once menacing and playful. Barlow's restless invented forms stretch the limits of mass, volume and height as they block, straddle and balance precariously. The audience is challenged into a new relationship with the sculptural object, the gallery environment and the world beyond. Barlow exhibited extensively across institutions internationally, including: Museum of Contemporary Art, Toronto (2023); Public Art Fund, New York (2023); Chillida Leku, Hernani (2023); Sprengel Museum, Hannover (2022); ARTIST ROOMS, Tate Modern, London (2021); Haus der Kunst, Munich (2021); Royal Academy of Arts, London (2019); La Biennale di Venezia, British Pavilion, Venice (2017); Kunsthalle Zurich, Zurich (2016); Nasher Sculpture Center, Dallas (2015); and Duveen Commission at Tate Britain, London (2014). Barlow was awarded the Niedersächsische Sparkassenstiftung's Kurt Schwitters Prize in 2022.

Olivia Bax (Singapore, b.1988) lives and works in London. She studied for a BA in Fine Art at the Byam Shaw School of Art, London (2007–10) and an MFA in Sculpture at the Slade School of Fine Art, London (2014–16). She was a Henry Moore Institute Research Fellow in 2023, where she researched and wrote the essay for this book. Bax was the winner of the Mark Tanner Sculpture Award (2019–20) and the Kenneth Armitage Young Sculptor Prize (2016). Her work is part of private and public collections, including: Arts Council Collection, UK; The Ingram Collection, London; and Tremenheere Sculpture Gardens, Penzance. Bax is a Lecturer of Fine Art at the University of Gloucestershire.

John Hoyland (b.1934, Sheffield – d.2011, London) was one of the most inventive and dynamic abstract painters of the post-war period. His dramatic and visually intense art evolved continually over the course of more than half a century. Retrospectives were held at the Royal Academy, London (1999) and Tate St Ives (2006). Posthumous solo exhibitions include *Power Stations*, Newport Street Gallery (2015), *The Last Paintings*, Sheffield Museums (2021) and *The Doors of Perception*, Mark Rothko Art Centre, Daugavpils (2023). His paintings are held in more than 50 public collections across the world.

Hew Locke (Edinburgh, UK, b.1959) spent his formative years (1966–80) in Guyana before returning to the UK to complete an MA in Sculpture at the Royal College of Art, London (1994). Locke's practice addresses the symbolism of statuary, monarchy and ships; how different cultures fashion their identities through visual symbols of authority; and how these representations are altered by the passage of time. Across an extensive and complex practice, Locke remains dedicated to illuminating histories, highlighting the relevance of the past within the context of contemporary culture and politics. Using various motifs, Locke reassesses the figureheads and imagery that represent nationhood. His critique of existing power structures is subtle and open-ended, encouraging the viewer to look more closely.

Anna Reading (Newcastle upon Tyne, UK, b.1987) lives and works in London. She holds an MFA in Sculpture from the Slade School of Fine Art and a BA in Fine Art from Central Saint Martins, London. Reading's sculptural practice combines a wide range of processes and materials, to explore novel ecosystems and science-fiction landscapes. Reading was the winner of the Mark Tanner Sculpture Award (2018–19).

Jessi Reaves (Portland, USA, b.1986) lives and works in New York. She is known for her multifaceted sculptural practice that approaches furniture as both material and subject, laying to waste the line between the functional and the aesthetic. Reaves has been the subject of solo exhibitions at institutions including: Arts Club of Chicago; Contemporary Arts Museum Houston; Carnegie Museum of Art, Pittsburgh; and Aldrich Contemporary Art Museum, Ridgefield. Her work is in the collections of the Brandhorst Museum, Munich; Hammer Museum, Los Angeles; Whitney Museum of American Art, New York; and Carnegie Museum of Art, among others.

Andrew Sabin (London, UK, b.1959) is an experimental sculptor who lives and works in West Sussex. His activities include object making, installation, public realm work and teaching. He is co-director of the Mattblackbarn education programme.

John Summers (Colorado, USA, b.1974) lives and works in London. Studying at the Slade School of Fine Art and then at the Royal College of Art (Sculpture School), he was a recipient of the Mark Tanner Sculpture Award in 2006, has shown in New Contemporaries and Zabludowicz Invites, and has work in several private collections nationally and internationally.

Chiffon Thomas's (Chicago, USA, b.1991) multifaceted practice incorporates embroidery, collage, drawing and sculpture to explore the self as split, fractured and transforming. Thomas contends with the crafted body in his work, examining wider issues of gender, race and sexuality. Thomas holds an MFA from Yale University and a BFA from the School of the Art Institute of Chicago. He has completed prominent residencies with the Skowhegan School of Painting and Sculpture and the Fountainhead Residency, Miami. His work is in the permanent collections of the Studio Museum in Harlem, New York; Hammer Museum, Los Angeles; Institute of Contemporary Art, Miami; Pérez Art Museum, Miami; and Currier Museum of Art, Manchester, New Hampshire, among others. Thomas was a recipient of the Joan Mitchell Fellowship in 2022. Thomas is represented by P.P.O.W. in New York and the Kohn Gallery in Los Angeles.

These Mad Hybrids:
John Hoyland and Contemporary Sculpture

This book was published on the occasion of an
exhibition of the same name at:

Royal West of England Academy (RWA), Bristol,
3 February–12 May 2024

Millennium Galleries, Sheffield,
20 February–18 May 2025

Exhibition curated by Olivia Bax, Sam Cornish
and Wiz Patterson Kelly

Published by Ridinghouse and Slimvolume, 2024
Publishers: Andrew Hunt and Sophie Kullmann

Edited by Olivia Bax, Sam Cornish, Andrew Hunt,
Sophie Kullmann and Wiz Patterson Kelly
Copy-edited and proofread by: Aimee Selby,
Linda Schofield and Georgia Spickett-Jones

Design: Michael Dyer, Remake
Production: Sophie Kullmann
Printed and bound by Verona Libri

We are most grateful to Mike Dyer for his remarkable flair for design
and great attention to detail, and to the team at Verona Libri for always delivering excellence in print. Thanks to Sam Cornish, Olivia
Bax and Wiz Patterson Kelly for always being a pleasure to work with.

For the book in this form © Ridinghouse and Slimvolume, 2024
Slimvolume #28

ISBN 978-1-910516-30-0

© The artists, authors, editors and publishers. All rights reserved.
No part of this book may be reproduced or transmitted in any form
or by any means, electronic or mechanical, including photocopy-
ing, recording or any other information storage or retrieval system,
without prior permission in writing from the publishers.

Distributed by Ridinghouse in the UK, Europe and the rest of the
world by
ACC Art Books
Sandy Lane, Old Martlesham
Woodbridge, Suffolk IP12 4SD
accartbooks.com

Distributed by Ridinghouse in the United States and Canada by
ARTBOOK / D.A.P.
75 Broad Street, Suite 630
New York, NY 10004
artbook.com

Distributed by Slimvolume via:

Slimvolume
57c Davisville Road
London W12 9SH
slimvolume.org

Cornerhouse Publications
HOME
2 Tony Wilson Place
Manchester M15 4FN
cornerhousepublications.org

Publication supported by the University of Gloucestershire, Royal
West of England Academy, Sheffield Museums Trust and the Henry
Moore Foundation

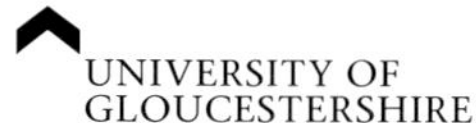

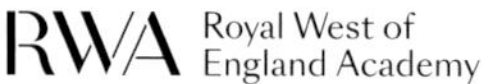

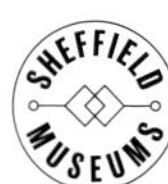

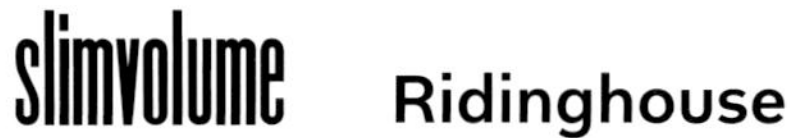

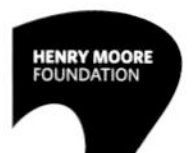